Dear Lucy

Dear Lucy

by

Tracey Evison

A diary written by a mother for her baby daughter
about her battle with the ATRT brain tumour.
(Atypical Teratoid Rhabdoid Tumour)

First published in Great Britain in 2016 by

Bannister Publications Ltd
118 Saltergate
Chesterfield
Derbyshire S40 1NG

ISBN 978-1-909813-21-2

Typeset in Palatino Linotype by Escritor Design, Chesterfield, Derbyshire

Printed and bound in Great Britain by SRP Ltd, Exeter, Devon

Helping Children with Cancer

PACT

PACT's association for Children
with Tumours and Leukaemia
Registered Charity No. 509012

All profits from the sale of this book will be donated to

PACT SHEFFIELD

(Parents' Association of Children with Tumours and Leukaemia)

PACT was founded in 1977, when eight parents created a support group for families whose children had cancer. The first donation was £113, encouraging PACT to raise funds for a Christmas party and a summer trip for the children. In 1978 the charity expanded its remit to include children with leukaemia and, as further funding was secured, its services grew to include the provision of equipment and facilities for families.

When the Charity was first launched, a child with cancer had a 55% chance of being alive 10 years after diagnosis. Today that chance has improved to more than 75%, but requiring prolonged and intensive treatment. Even so, it is sadly not always successful. PACT is an invaluable source of practical and emotional support for children and their families throughout their contact with hospital treatment teams.

PACT owns and runs a house in Sheffield, located next to the Sheffield Children's Hospital. Lucy's father, Paul, was able to use the house on many occasions: a precious gift that allowed him to stay close to Lucy and Tracey.

Over the last 30 years PACT has raised money to help support families, and increasingly to support the paediatric oncology ward and clinic at Sheffield Children's Hospital, as well as contributing to research. The charity recently launched an appeal to raise funds for a new Oncology and Haematology clinic at the hospital.

The new clinic will be next to Ward M3, where Lucy and others were treated. In addition to all the existing facilities it will have a new treatment suite and an improved waiting area for families. The clinic will be known as the 'PACT Children's Centre for Oncology and Haematology', and is expected to be ready for use in 2017. It will make a big difference to all the families that use it.

The appeal has a target of £670,000, to be raised over the next two years.

All profits from the sale of this book will be donated to the appeal.

Foreword

Many novels begin with a 'List of Characters' and as this book developed I began to think that perhaps I should do the same, for the story is about a big family, embracing more than brothers, sisters, aunts, uncles and grandparents; it now includes a great number of friends, medical professionals and people who have taken to their hearts the one focus of the tale, our daughter Lucy. The little girl whose beauty, courage, resilience and fortitude has changed all our lives and has brought us together.

Lucy Needham was born in September 2013, to her immensely proud parents – me, Tracey Evison, and my partner Paul Needham. Lucy joined our family with Paul's wonderful children, Jack and Molly. From our home near Chesterfield, Derbyshire, we looked forward to happy days and all the things that families anticipate in life. It was not to be that simple…

In August 2014, when Lucy was just 10 months old, our lives were turned upside down when she was diagnosed with a rare and aggressive brain tumour.

From the very beginning I kept a diary to record the messages of support we received and to describe what happened to Lucy and those around her. I always intended the diary to be solely for Lucy, but as it progressed I began to realise that other families experiencing the same journey might find in it some cause for hope and strength to carry on in the face of their own trials.

The initial prognosis for Lucy's condition (ATRT) is bleak and in the early days when I searched for positive stories I found very few. Lucy's journey is not yet over and she is still dealing with many side effects of the tumour and the subsequent treatment, but I feel that we are over the worst. I believe that Lucy has overcome her hardest fight and, proud of her beyond measure, I want to share her story to give hope to others.

I also hope that the book will raise funds for PACT (Parent's Association of Children with Tumours and Leukaemia), one of the many fantastic charities that have supported us.

It has been a deeply challenging experience, in which we have drawn heavily on each other's strength, patience and love. Paul continues to my rock, and the most wonderful Daddy that Lucy, Jack and Molly could ever ask for. Thank you, Paul, for always being there. My profound thanks go to Jack and Molly – the best big brother and big sister Lucy could ever want.

I would also like to thank Paul's mum, Sheena, for being the most wonderful Granny to Lucy, and my mum, Nannie Evison, for her continued love and support. I am especially grateful for all that they do for us.

This book would not have been possible without the help and support of my publisher, Tom Blyth, at Bannister Publications Ltd. To his name I would add many others whom I should like to single out for special thanks, if space allowed. However, readers will find their names and my reasons to thank them within the pages of the diary.

But my greatest thanks are reserved for Lucy, to whom this book is dedicated. I never realised I could love someone so much. You amaze me every day. I hope that in time, medical science will find ways to defeat this cruel disease. Until that day comes, we must never give up hope. Miracles really do happen.

How It Started

"Lucy needs emergency surgery. We will operate first thing tomorrow morning."

We were first admitted to the Chesterfield Royal Hospital on Friday 1 August 2014. A few days earlier you had had a particularly sickly day, and I contacted our health visitor to say that I was worried you might be getting dehydrated. She came to have a look at you and instantly asked us to take you to our local surgery in Wingerworth. We were able to see Dr Sid very quickly and I will never forget how kind and caring he was. He suggested that we take you to hospital for assessment by a paediatrician, who could find out why you were being sick. Dr Sid said they might keep you in overnight. This was utterly unexpected and it terrified me. What could be wrong with my beautiful little girl?

We stayed in the hospital for two nights on that occasion, but the staff didn't seem to be getting anywhere other than surmising that you might be allergic to milk. We were discharged and offered a different type of formula milk for you.

You continued to be sick the following week and by the Saturday night Daddy and I knew that there was something seriously wrong. I wasn't at all convinced it was a milk allergy. You were hardly eating, but frequently vomiting. I was very worried that you were becoming dehydrated. I decided to call 111 for advice. They quickly made an appointment for us at 10.45pm that night with the out-of-hours doctor at the Chesterfield Royal Hospital. You were fast asleep and part of me felt guilty for disturbing you, but I also knew I couldn't wait another night without getting medical help.

The out-of-hours doctor was very patient, but said again that it was probably the milk allergy and maybe we should just try a different sort of milk. He gave us the choice to go home and come back in the morning, but I wanted you to be checked out there and then.

So we were admitted to Nightingale Ward again, the second weekend running.

The doctors came to see you and ordered various tests. Cystic Fibrosis was even mentioned, because of the persistent cough that you had, but their main concern was the vomiting and your lack of nutrition. Every time you tried to eat or drink you would be instantly sick. So it was that you had your first NG tube (a neo-gastric feeding tube) inserted. It was a traumatic experience. I will never forget seeing you struggle as the nurses tried to insert the narrow tube into your tummy via the nose. You clearly hated it, but you were eating so little that you had to be fed your milk through the tube. Having the tube on your face suddenly made you look like a very sick child, and seemed to make it more serious. I can only imagine what it must have felt like for you. Some of the nurses have since told me that they practise inserting the tubes on each other, so they know how uncomfortable it can be. Little did I know that this would be the first of many NG tubes you would have inserted and how it would become something you and I truly hated. You would gag every time but I had to tell myself that it was helping you stay alive.

We were in the hospital over the whole weekend. On the Monday, one of the doctors decided to order an ultrasound scan of your head. She assumed that it had been done already, but I said, "No, why would we look at Lucy's head if this was a milk allergy?" The scan showed some excess fluid on the brain and enlarged ventricles. The doctor immediately went to telephone the neurosurgeons at Sheffield Children's Hospital. She returned to say that an ambulance would be here within four hours to take you to Sheffield. The neurosurgeons would investigate the ultrasound results. You would need to have an MRI scan immediately, but Chesterfield didn't have any available slots for several days. Daddy and I were dazed by this turn of events; everything suddenly became very frightening. I remember ringing

'Ventricles'
There are four ventricles in the brain, forming a set of communicating cavities, filled with cerebrospinal fluid, which bathes the central nervous system.

2

Nannie in panic, not knowing what to think, or do.

We arrived at Sheffield Children's Hospital that evening, and placed on S2 Ward (the Neurosciences Ward for patients who have issues affecting the brain). You would have a CT scan the following morning (a computerised tomography (CT) scan uses X-rays and a computer to create detailed images of the inside of the body). They were going to do this first and then run a MRI scan afterwards if necessary (magnetic resonance imaging (MRI) is a type of scan that uses strong magnetic fields and radio waves to produce detailed images of the inside of the body). You were sick several times in the night and I remember being more frightened than I have ever felt in my life. What on earth was wrong with my precious little girl?

Once the CT scan had been done we waited with you in one of the bays on S2 Ward. The consultant was very busy and seemed to avoid making eye contact with us. I remember thinking, doesn't she know how painful this waiting is? Can't she do those jobs later and just come and talk to us with the results? Of course, it was selfish, but we were so very anxious. She was extremely busy because she was putting everything in place for you. She knew that you would need emergency surgery and couldn't come and talk to us without the other members of the team being present, and she was trying to arrange all of that too.

It was a few hours later when she finally ushered us into a room and it was when several other people followed us into the room, one with a box of tissues, that I suddenly began to panic. This definitely wasn't 'just a milk allergy' anymore.

She explained that the CT scan had confirmed an excess amount of fluid on the brain and that the ventricles were enlarged. "However," she said, "we spotted something else too, which took us by surprise... there is quite a large mass. Here, you can see," she said, pointing to a grey blurry image on the computer screen. I couldn't really see what she was looking at and I repeated what she had said, "A mass, what do you mean, a mass? Do you mean a... do you mean a tumour?"

"Yes," she said. "Lucy needs emergency surgery. We will operate first thing tomorrow morning."

The Diary begins...

The First Operation

✦

Removing the Tumour

Tuesday 12 August 2014

It was the most devastating news imaginable. Lucy, our gorgeous, precious ten-month-old daughter had a brain tumour and the surgeons at Sheffield Children's Hospital needed to operate immediately.

Wednesday 13 August 2014

So began the longest day of our lives. After lots of cuddles and kisses we left you early in the morning in the hands of the surgeons. They were still strangers to us and I was putting your life in their hands. I found it so hard handing you over to them, not quite knowing what they were going to find. I couldn't really speak but I remember just saying, "Please, please look after her". Daddy and I walked away in tears, not knowing what to do with ourselves. We had been told by the surgeons that we may as well stay away from hospital until at least 5pm. That seemed like a lifetime away. You would be under anaesthetic all that time and we knew how dangerous that was. It just didn't seem real. Just a few days ago the doctors and consultants at Chesterfield Royal Hospital were still talking about a possible milk allergy… and now this?

A couple of weeks previous to this day you had become rather poorly and you were often sick most mornings. You became quite lethargic too and you didn't seem to have much energy to do anything. It felt like something was wrong but other than these symptoms there were no indication of just how poorly you actually were. For the first ten months you had been a happy healthy baby. You had transformed my life and I had never been so happy. Daddy dotes on you too, as do Jack and Molly, your half-brother and half-sister, who spend a great deal of time with us. You filled our days with joy and happiness and we had so much fun every day meeting new friends, both for you and me. There were several baby groups that we went to and if we didn't have one of those groups planned for the day ahead then we would usually meet up with our neighbours that we had made friends with. Little Ioan was born just six days before you and so his mummy, Sian, and I have become very close. It was lovely to have such good friends living close by.

We wandered into Sheffield city centre not really knowing what to do. We bought a 'Get Well Soon' card and a special teddy for you. Other than that I don't really remember what we did. We returned to the Children's Hospital and at about 6pm we were told that the operation was over and that you would start to wake up very soon. You will never know what a frightening time this was for us. We knew you were still going to be very poorly when you woke up. As soon as the buzzer sounded on the pager, I ran towards the operating theatre doors.

We had to wait in a side room for a short time until the consultant came to see us. He seemed pleased, saying that they had removed quite a large mass from your brain, but there was a little bit left that they couldn't touch as it was too dangerous. He said that to do so might result in permanent brain damage, and that they would need to do further pathological tests in the laboratory before they could determine the nature of the tumour. It would be ten agonising days before we would find out what this mass was and whether it was cancerous. "You must know. Why can't you tell us now?" I remember asking,

At that moment all I wanted to do was see you. We were taken to the recovery area and there you were. I burst into tears when I saw you. My little girl, with her head all bandaged up, and wires here there and everywhere. It all looked so frightening. I held your hand and told you I loved you. You looked so sleepy. Did that mean you were OK? Should you be awake by now? I threw all these questions at the nurses and the anaesthetist. They were so calm and reassuring. One of the nurses, Karen, is often with you when you have to go back to theatre again, and she is so kind. I always feel better knowing she has been with you, as she has from the very beginning. She knows your special toy, 'Cow Cow', that came on this very first trip to theatre with you. It's a highland cow that came from Scotland as a present from Daddy when he visited there. It's not the cutest of soft toys but it was a present from Daddy and it has been on every trip to theatre with you since.

What happened next is a bit of a blur. I remember feeling emotionally exhausted. You were moved to the High Dependency Unit (HDU), where you would have one-to-one nursing care. The staff on the HDU are absolutely amazing and we will be forever grateful to them. The sights and sounds of that enormous room will never leave me. Brightly lit, it always feels like daytime and the bleeps and the machines don't stop. I remember looking around and thinking how poorly all of the other little children were and then I looked at you and realised you were now one of them. The next few days would be critical to see how your body coped after the major surgery. I couldn't quite believe we were here, but I was at your bedside day and night.

And this is how the idea of the diary began. For much of the day I would sit at your bedside, and the days seemed very long. Doctors and nurses were always rushing over to check one thing or another. The nurses in HDU had to record all sorts of statistics on the enormous grid sheets at the end of the bed. None of it made any sense to me.

One of the things that kept me going was reading all the messages of love and support in text messages or on Facebook. I hadn't put much on Facebook initially as we only told our friends and family about your condition, but now it became a lifeline. Being able to read friends' words of encouragement, love and support really kept me going.

One of those dear friends is Tamara. I work with her and we once shared an office. I think she would agree that we were work colleagues rather than close friends; but since you were admitted to hospital Tamara has been my absolute rock. She sends me messages me every day to ask how we are or to tell me some random story about her lovely son, Jake. I think it is to distract me, but I appreciate it. She has also done very many kind things for us – too many to list here, but you'll notice in the diary just how many times she crops up and how many gifts and presents we received from her. I will never forget what an amazing friend she has been to us - truly wonderful. She suddenly appeared on the HDU one day, bringing a card, a guardian angel to look over you and a little notebook to write down all the messages of love and support from friends and family so that you could look back and read them one day. That's exactly what I did and the messages quickly evolved into a daily diary. Once I had finished the first notebook, I started another…. and another….

Saturday 16 August 2014

We have been on the HDU since Wednesday evening. We are by your bedside all the time. You are still having difficulties with your breathing but you are staying awake for longer periods of time and you have started to reach for your toys and Daddy's nose. Mummy had her first cuddle in days. It was so emotional but absolutely lovely. I was scared at first as I didn't want to damage any of the wires or pull them out. The nurses were so kind and patient, and helped me to do it carefully. I think they knew how important it was to have that first cuddle. I was desperate to hold you as soon as you came back from theatre on Wednesday night, but I've been waiting for three long days instead. I had cuddled you every day since you were born and I was worried that you might be wondering why I wasn't doing so now.

Your brother and sister, Jack and Molly, have visited too. It was important for them to see their baby sister as they love you dearly and have done so from the moment they first saw you. It has been a very frightening time for them and they have been very brave. It is hard to know how much to tell them, but they know that you had an operation on your head to remove a lump that shouldn't be there, and that you are very, very poorly. We've also told them that the doctors and nurses are doing all they can to make you better as quickly as possible but that you might be in hospital for a while yet.

My Uncle Gary brought Nannie from Skegness to see you. It was upsetting for her and for us, but I am glad she came. I didn't know she was coming; she just appeared one afternoon on the HDU. Granny has been to see you too, as have Uncle Mark and Auntie Alison. You are so deeply loved by all of your family, not just Mummy and Daddy… xxx

A couple of nights ago, about 9pm, the fire alarm sounded. Daddy had gone up to his room in Treetops (the accommodation for the parents of very sick children, which is managed by a fabulous charity called The Sick Children's Trust). At the sound of the alarm, I just froze. With all the wires and monitors around you, how on earth were they going to evacuate you and all the other sick children?

I began to panic and the nurses must have seen my reaction. They were calm and professional and tried to reassure me. "It's OK", they said, "We've done this before. Everyone will be fine." Quickly but calmly, they gathered bits and pieces from around the room and placed some items in the cot. They couldn't possibly move us now? You needed all this equipment? I didn't know what I should take with me. The only thing that was important was you. Then two firemen walked into the HDU, announcing that a toaster had set off the alarms and we didn't need to be evacuated. A toaster! I was nearly hysterical with fear, all because of a toaster.

The HDU soon returned to its normal buzz and five minutes later it was as if nothing had happened. I tried to calm down, resuming my usual position in the chair by your bed, and took out the little notebook that Tamara had brought me earlier in the day. She brought me a guardian angel to look over you, a lovely card and a little notebook for me to keep a record of all the messages we were receiving. It was a shock to see her today and I cried as she hugged me. I couldn't really speak. But I think the notebook will really help me.

Here are some of the messages we have received already:

★ Special challenges are only given to those tough enough to cope with them. Go Lucy! The bravest little girl I know. (Sian)

★ Thinking of you all the time. (Granny)

★ She is such a brave and strong little girl. We are thinking of you all. (Sonja and Mikey)

★ A fighter! She's such a strong lady like her Mummy! (Michelle, one of Mummy's friends at work)

★ She's such a feisty fighter... like her mum. (Jo, one of Mummy's old work friends)

★ Come on Lucy, we are with you all the way. (Jill, from Mummy's work)

★ Sending Lucy every bit of positive energy and love I can find. I have been thinking about you so, so much. Big hugs and cuddles. (Fiona, Mummy's work friend)

★ Keep your head up. God gives his hardest battles to his strongest soldiers. (Tamara)

★ Ioan is missing his beautiful friend and looking forward to getting up to all sorts of mischief soon. (Sian)

★ Keep fighting Lucy! We are all thinking of you and sending hugs and prayers. (Kaz, a 'Waterbaby mummy', from the swimming group that we used to attend)

★ Come on now little Lucy and show us how strong you are sweetheart. (Sandy, one of Mummy's work friends)

Sunday 17 August 2014

Today you were moved from the HDU, back to the neurology ward, S2. You have been making good progress. You no longer need help with your breathing and the amount of drugs you need has been reduced.

Complications

✦

Inserting an External Ventricular Drain

Monday 18 August 2014

Last night didn't go quite to plan and overnight you developed a large lump on the back of your head, like a big swollen golf ball. This gradually increased during the night. This morning the doctors said that, following the operation, you were failing to drain the excess fluid from your brain yourself and would need some help. You would need immediate surgery to insert an 'External Ventricular Drain'. It is basically a plastic tube that drains fluid from the ventricles of the brain and thus keeps them decompressed.

'External Ventricular Drain'

A device used to relieve a build-up of fluid on the brain: hydrocephalus. The excess fluid puts pressure on the brain, which can cause damage when the normal flow of cerebrospinal fluid around the brain is obstructed.

We couldn't believe you were going to have to endure another operation so soon. We felt so sad and scared. You look so tiny and it just doesn't seem fair. Daddy and I just wished we could have the operations for you. However, the operation was completed relatively quickly and we were back on the ward recovering with you quite soon after.

I am now sitting on the ward with you and watching you sleeping peacefully. I feel frightened looking at the piece of equipment next to your bed, knowing how critical it is for you.

I am scared of touching it, but the nurses check the levels regularly. Seeing the tube coming directly out of your head is surreal. Surely you are too little for this. I've only just got used to the monitor attached to you that records your heart rate and oxygen saturations. I watch the numbers go up and down, bleeping if they get too high or too low, which they often do and the nurses come rushing over. Now there is something else to stare at. I just hope that it is doing what it needs to do to help you.

Tuesday 19 August 2014

Lots of our friends and family have been sending messages of love and support on Facebook or by text. So many people are worrying about you and hoping you will get better very soon. We will tell you all about these difficult challenges that you have endured when you are older. But I am writing lots of the messages down for now for you to read in years to come. We love you so very much…

★ 'Bless her. She's a little fighter! Sending big kisses for Lucy.' (Helen, Dave, Ella and Isabel)

★ 'Give Lucy loads of kisses and hugs for a brave little girl.' (Grandpa Geoff, Nanna Kaz, Steph and Selina)

★ 'She's amazing. Big love as always.' (Jen)

★ 'She is amazing. Love her so very much.' (Sian)

★ Be brave little Lucy. We are all sending you lots of love and kisses. Keep strong Lucy and Mummy and Daddy. (Debs, Paul and Isabelle)

★ 'She is such a brave girl. Lots of love.' (Becky, Ben and Ruby)

★ 'Hope Lucy is ok. She's a fantastic little fighter. Lots of love to you all.' (Donna, Matt, Ben and Oliver)

The neurosurgeons Mr McCullen and Mrs Patricia de Lacy, and the other doctors and nurses are looking after us too. Patricia even bought us some croissants for breakfast today. She was the first to break the news to us about the tumour, and she was also there on the morning of the main operation. She has been so lovely. She has a little girl herself, not much older than you, so it feels like she can really relate to what we are going through. I will always remember her kindness.

Wednesday 20 August 2014

You smiled at us today! Daddy and I were so happy we cried – no wonder you didn't give us a second smile.

The days seem so long. Daddy and I are by your bedside constantly, talking to you and touching you and hoping that you'll soon start to respond. You are on fairly high doses of morphine and so you just spend most of the day sleeping. You can't sit up yet. We just want our little girl back, and hopefully that gorgeous smile that you've just given us is the first step.

Something cheered me up today – a special card from some of the mums and babies from one of our baby groups. It is a very big card that they have made, with all your friends' handprints on it. We will treasure it forever. I am so touched by their kindness. Many of them have bought you lovely presents too - a stripy horse from Benjamin and a doggy from Henry, to name just two. The toys are sitting in the cot, waiting for you to play with them or give them a cuddle.

Thursday 21 August 2014

You have become a little dehydrated today, from losing so much fluid from your drain and not managing to replace enough with your feeds. You need to have another tube (a cannula) fitted so that they can give you some fluids. The doctors are struggling to find a vein so they may have to put you under anaesthetic again to have a special one fitted. You yelped as they tried to insert the needles. I couldn't bear to watch. Is there not an easier way?

Daddy and I are also feeling very nervous today, expecting to receive the results about the tumour. Is it cancerous or not? We are preparing ourselves for the worse and we will tackle whatever we need to deal with.

We have been assigned a Community Nurse, Rachel Ducker, who is our key worker. She comes to see us most days. She is absolutely lovely, like a mother hen. Both Daddy and I are upset most of the time, but as soon as we start to talk about what has happened, Rachel is just great. She listens, hugs, holds my hand and I know she is there for us. Although we don't really know her, we know she is here to try to make things easier for us at this unbearable time. We ask her so many questions and she answers was fully as she can, but I also detect that she is very careful not to say

'Everything will be OK'.

Friday 22 August 2014

I don't know what to write. There are no words. I can't believe what the doctors have just told us. Maybe tomorrow I'll have the energy to write more.

Diagnosis

✦

Fear of the 'Known Unknowns'

Sunday 24 August 2014

On Friday the doctors told us that the tumour in your brain was cancerous. It is a rare, malignant and fast growing tumour, called an Atypical Teratoid Rhabdoid Tumour (ATRT) and it was located in the Posterior Fossa region of the brain. To be honest, I don't care what it is called or where it was. We are heartbroken.

Googling hasn't done us any favours. Less than 10% of the under-three's survive ATRT and only 1% of all paediatric brain tumours are ATRT. But I have found a couple of success stories and we are hanging onto those. The nurses tell me not to but I sit looking on the internet all the time, often into the early hours of the morning when I can't sleep, desperately searching for more success stories of children who have had this tumour. I just want to know as much as possible because if I don't know then I can't ask the doctors the right questions.

Ironically, this was the day that Auntie Claire and Uncle Ben travelled all the way from Cardiff to see us. Just as we were walking into the consultant's room to discuss the results, Claire and Ben appeared at the hospital doors. I couldn't speak to them then, but when we came out of the room, obviously upset, Claire and Ben were there by the cot with you. Claire hugged me and I remember saying to her, "Lucy might die"; words you never imagine having to say to your big sister about your daughter, their little niece. I have not said those words again and I never will. You are going to beat this Lucy and you'll be reading all about this in years to come.

The struggle you're in today is developing the strength
you need for tomorrow.

One thing that is taking my mind off everything is trying to raise some sponsorship for our dear friends Sian, Katie and Sarah. They have decided to enter the Sheffield 10k run to raise money for the Sick Children's Trust and for Macmillan Nurses. These are two absolutely fantastic charities. The Sick Children's Trust funds residential accommodation in hospitals for families of seriously ill patients, and here at Sheffield we call it Treetops. Daddy has been given the use of one of their rooms and he sleeps there for a few hours overnight, as we can only have one parent sleep by your bed. I also use the room for showering and freshening up and as somewhere to keep my clothes.

It has been invaluable and we are so pleased our friends want to raise some money for them. I put a simple request on Facebook asking for friends to donate and in less than 24 hours the total already stands at over £500. I am delighted. I will be too busy helping to look after you to do the run myself, and I have never been any good at running, but I want to do something to raise money for these charities. I would also like to support the Sheffield Children's Hospital Charity along with other cancer charities and in particular those that focus on children's brain tumours and on support for families.

But for now, I just need to keep busy and focus on how we are going to get you better. And we will Lucy. We will. Love you lots little Lucy... xxx

Never stop believing in HOPE because MIRACLES happen every day.

Monday 25 August 2014

Today is Daddy's 37th birthday. It is a very strange birthday for him. I feel sad because I've been unable to buy him presents as I normally would, but I have managed to get him a couple of small things from the museum shop close to the hospital. Jack and Molly are visiting later and they have promised to bring Daddy a birthday cake. You very thoughtfully gave Daddy probably the best birthday present he could wish for this year – an enormous smile and a giggle. The play therapist brought you some fibre optical lights for your cot and you love watching the lights flicker. They seem to capture your attention, if even just for a few moments... another glimpse of how our little Lucy used to be.

We are also meeting the oncologist today to discuss treatment. I have no idea what is involved or how long you will need to have treatment. I have so many questions I don't know where to begin or what to ask first. We are determined to stay positive and while there are still things we can do, we believe you can still get better. Anyway, statistics are just pointless when you are that 1%.

You will be 11 months old tomorrow and we have already planned your 1st Birthday party. Most of the invitations went out a couple of weeks ago. Now we need to make you strong enough to enjoy the party.

Dr Vicki Lee will be our lead oncology consultant. We met her yesterday. I knew your prognosis was bleak but I don't think I realised quite how bleak. She said, "It's not like there isn't anything we can do, we will try to do something." I think that was supposed to be reassuring but it sounded so desperate. ATRT is a particularly nasty tumour and has a very high chance of reoccurrence. The neurosurgeons were unable to completely remove the tumour and there is a small patch still remaining. They say that it is very, very tiny, but it is still there. It is separate to the main tumour. Chemo-therapy will hopefully kill it off, but there is every chance it could grow back. The tumour is a fast growing one too, so things would happen quickly if it did return.

You are too young for radiation. You will be given a course of chemotherapy, three cycles every 2-3 weeks. Then you will need to have something called high-dose chemotherapy and a stem cell transplant. This approach to treatment will give you the best possible chance of fighting the disease. All of this is a whole new language to me and I am frantically trying to take it all in. You will be given an array of drugs that I have never heard of. I don't think I managed to write all of them down but the consultant mentioned Doxorubicin, Vincristine, Ifosfamide, Cyclophosphamide, Etoposide, Carboplatin, and a high dose of Thiotepa. It sounded such a cocktail of toxic drugs.

You would have a lumbar puncture (an injection into your spine) every fortnight for some of the drugs, under general anaesthetic, which would mean regular trips to theatre. The regular trips to theatre present a risk: will your body cope with all that anaesthetic? It felt like information overload and I was desperately trying to write things down and trying to take it all in. My hands were shaking. This was terrifying.

Sometimes we just have to stand back and let life happen and trust that it will work out.

Wednesday 27 August 2014

Today you are going to have your third operation, to have something called a Ventriculoperitoneal Shunt fitted. This will be permanent and you will have it for the rest of your life. I find those words so scary to hear. It will drain away excess fluid from your brain. The tube passes all the way into your abdomen. It will be visible on the back of your head but in time your hair will cover it.

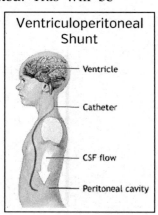

Ventriculoperitoneal Shunt

Ventricle

Catheter

CSF flow

Peritoneal cavity

The operation will take about three hours. It will feel like a lifetime to us. I hate watching you being put to sleep and I find it very upsetting. 'Cow Cow' is ready to go with you.

You are also going to have a Portacath fitted to enable you to receive all the chemotherapy drugs. This is instead of having a cannula. It is a small appliance that is installed beneath the skin on your upper chest. A catheter then connects the port to a vein.

It will take a few days for you to recover from the operation and then you will possibly be moved to the Oncology Ward (M3) to begin your first round of chemo. The nurses keep suggesting we go and visit M3. They said it would be good for us to see how friendly the ward is, before you are moved there. It will reassure you, they said. I just kept thinking I didn't want to see the ward. I had images in my head of what it might be like - a ward full of children receiving cancer treatment. And Lucy would soon be one of them. My little girl would be treated for cancer?

Thursday 28 August 2014

You had a lovely surprise today: a gorgeous teddy bear has arrived from your friends Ioan, Thomas, Oliver, Millie, Ruby and Oliver. The teddy has a special message on his t-shirt that says, 'We love you Lucy'. It is absolutely gorgeous and will take pride of place in your cot.

Friday 29 August 2014

Helen and Nannie are visiting later from Skegness, but we have just been told you will shortly be heading back to theatre again. They need to fit another line for some of the chemo and the only chance they have got to do it is today. We thought it wasn't going to be until Monday. So another busy day…

Daddy and I are going to try to be brave and will visit M3 while you are in theatre. It seems a good time to go…

I think we'll be moving to M3 tomorrow. We'll be sad to leave S2, as all the nurses and neurosurgeons have been fabulous. You have become particularly fond of Kat and Ella, and we will be eternally grateful to them for caring for our precious little girl. They have been wonderful. You love Ella and you always give her a big smile. I hope the nurses are just as nice on M3.

Discovering Ward M3

✦

Our New Home-from-Home

Saturday 30 August 2014

So here we are on the new ward, M3. We actually have our own room! I have been busy putting up all your cards, and pictures from Molly. The doctors have just removed your big head bandage and it is lovely to see you without it. As I write, you are having a blood transfusion. I had no idea what this entailed, and thought it would be much more complicated than it actually is. I see how much easier it is to have the Portacath fitted, as they just connect everything to it. They call it 'Mr Wiggly' to try and make it fun for the children. You are happily sleeping through it while the machine pumps blood into your body, to replace the blood you lost during surgery. Amazing! I will be making sure I go to donate blood as soon as I can.

Jack, Molly, Granny, Auntie Helen and Uncle James will be visiting tomorrow. We're looking forward to seeing them. They are missing you. We were supposed to be on holiday in Dorset this week. Never mind, the five of us will make it there one day. I'm sure of it. We are not having much luck with family holidays. Last year, when I was pregnant with you, we had a week away in North Devon. We had a wonderful couple of days and then Daddy fell ill with pneumonia, and ended up in Barnstaple hospital on the Thursday and Friday night.

We are still receiving lots of 'Get Well Soon' cards for you. Daddy has been home today and picked up some more post. Miranda's granny has knitted you some lovely little booties - they are super cute. I will be keeping all your cards and special presents in a memory box so that you'll be able to look at them when you are older. You have been given a certificate each time you have been to theatre and they are on the wall here. You have four certificates already. I'm hoping you don't get many more.

I don't know how my story will end, but nowhere in the text will it ever read "I gave up".

Sunday 31 August 2014

You have had such a good day today. Lots of giggles and smiles for me and Daddy and Hannah the nurse. You do this cute little scrunched up nose thing that Hannah adores. She always hopes you will do it for her when she comes into the room.

Hannah was our nurse yesterday and is still with us today. As soon as we met her, I felt reassured that the nurses here on M3 were just as amazing and caring as those on S2. I'm not quite sure why I felt they would be any different. M3 must be one of the most challenging places to work in the hospital. I think I had put so much trust in the nurses and neurosurgeons on S2 that I didn't think anyone else would be as good. Sheffield Children's Hospital is a very special place, particularly M3, and all of the doctors and nurses, every single one of them, are fantastic. The things they have to deal with day in and day out… and they work such long hours, often three days in a row, on 12-hour shifts. But they look after one another and all the families who walk through the door. It's like one big family. I am so emotional all of the time… I don't know how they put up with me.

You can almost sit up on your own today. We have put a mat on the floor with lots of toys and you have been happily playing with them. You also have a special blue chair from the physio team and you have been sitting up in that too. Daddy and I are going to have a little treat for tea today as we are so fed up with hospital café food. We're going to have an Indian meal, delivered to A&E. That's something I never imagined we would be doing.

Monday 1 September 2014

Today should have been my first day back at work after maternity leave. I work as a School Improvement Officer for Literacy in North Lincolnshire. I used to be a primary school teacher but I now work for the Local Education Authority supporting the teachers. (I've probably told you all this by the time you are reading this.) Daddy also needs to go to his new job today. He was supposed to start there two weeks ago. He's very upset about leaving you and I know that it's going to be very difficult for him. I don't really want him to leave us but I know he must work.

Today is another big day for you! They are bringing a special machine into your room for collecting some of your stem cells. The cells are stored and then transplanted back into your body after the high-dose chemotherapy. They call it a 'stem cell harvest'. It will take about four hours and two specialist nurses will be with us all day. I am a bit nervous about it but I have learnt to trust these amazing doctors and nurses, and I'm sure it will be OK. And you have been so very brave already.

'Stem Cell Harvesting'

A drip is inserted into each arm and attaches to a machine. Blood passes out of one drip, through the machine and back into the body through the other drip.

The machine filters the stem cells out of the blood. The stem cells are collected and frozen until the patient is ready to have them back.

Tuesday 2 September 2014

The first attempt at the stem cell harvest didn't quite go to plan yesterday so they've got to try it again today. Another four hours of the noisy machine.

On a more positive note, Daddy and I were allowed to take you for a quick walk around the park yesterday evening. It was a warm summer's evening and you enjoyed watching the ducks. Uncle Mark, Auntie Alison and Katie came to join us. It was the first time you had been outside since 11th August.

Sian came to visit today, bringing me a very special present, a Pandora charm bracelet. I've always wanted one of these. It also has my first charm on it – a little duckling to remind me of our walks with Ioan and Lucy around Stubbing Court in Wingerworth, where we live. It will help me to look forward to our first walk to see the ducks when we are home again. We are so lucky to have friends like Sian, Ioan and Liam.

Jack and Molly are coming later. Daddy is picking them up from their Grandma's house and then they are coming straight here. I'm hoping we'll be able to go out for walk with the pushchair again.

Wednesday 3 September

Jack and Molly have been invited to a special 'Sibling Day' on the 4th October. It is being organised by the charity, CLIC Sargent, to help brothers and sisters to deal understand why you are here and what the doctors and nurses are doing to make you better. I do hope they'll want to come. There will be various activities for them to do that will help them understand more about that dreaded word, 'cancer'. Of course, Daddy and I have tried to talk to Jack and Molly, but it is so hard to talk about it without getting upset ourselves. I don't think they would want to go on their own, but as they have each other for support, I think they'll be OK.

Something else that has cheered me up today is finding out that two of our friends, Becky and Julie from one of the baby groups we used to go to, organised an impromptu coffee morning and raised £126 for a charity of our choice. How unbelievably kind of them. I was overwhelmed when I read their message. We have decided to choose CLIC Sargent as they have been supporting us since we first got here and a social worker comes to visit us most days. It's great

CLIC Sergeant - the UK's leading cancer charity for children and young people, and their families.

CLIC Sargent provides clinical, practical, financial and emotional support to help them cope with cancer and get the most out of life. We are there from diagnosis onwards and aim to help the whole family deal with the impact of cancer and its treatment, life after treatment and, in some cases, bereavement.

CLIC Sargent was formed in 2005 after a successful merger between CLIC and Sargent Cancer Care for Children.

Sargent Cancer Care for Children - founded in 1968 by Sylvia Darley OBE as a lasting memory to the late Sir Malcolm Sargent.

CLIC - Cancer and Leukaemia in Childhood - founded in 1976 in the south west by Bob Woodward following the diagnosis of his young son Robert with cancer two years before. Sadly, Robert died in 1977 aged 11 years, and Bob went on to dedicate his life to charity work.

we can support them.

Not much else is happening today: possibly another attempt at the stem cell harvest if they didn't get enough yesterday and maybe an Echocardiogram (ECHO) of your heart too... and a kidney test. So maybe there is a lot going on!

The physiotherapists have brought you another special chair but you are already sitting up on your own. You have been doing so in your cot this morning while playing with your toys. It has been lovely to see.

Thursday 4 September

You should be starting chemotherapy today but it has been postponed until tomorrow so that they can try one more day of stem cell harvesting. I am worried about the possible consequences of delaying the chemotherapy. We have been told that you have a fast-growing tumour. What if it has started growing again already and it will be too late for chemotherapy to have any effect? It is frightening.

I feel very sad today because we need to cancel your 1st Birthday party. We had planned a big party at Wingerworth Church Centre, with about 70 friends and family invited, and I was so looking forward to it, as were Jack and Molly. It was going to be a special party for you with all our family and friends, instead of having you christened, with us not being particularly religious. But we think it would be too overwhelming for everyone and, most importantly, for you. So we have decided to cancel it for now but we plan on having a big celebration when you are feeling better.

A wonderful charity, called the Pippa Jones Little Treasure Trust, has donated a bag of terrific toys for you. One of the play therapists has just delivered it to you room. It has some Duplo, a soft toy, an Elmer book and a wooden ladybird toy. It is as if someone knew we needed something to make us smile a little today. Thank you to this brilliant charity.

Chemotherapy

✦

But Babies Don't Get Cancer Do They?

Friday 5 September 2014

We are just sitting in your room on M3 waiting to be called to theatre. This will be your fifth procedure in less than four weeks. They will be starting your chemotherapy today, too. I hope it doesn't make you feel sick, although they said it might. It is such a surreal day; one that I never imagined you would have to endure. Babies don't get cancer do they? That's what I used to think.

Something exciting happened on the ward today. A little baby was born! A pregnant mum was here with her three-year-old, who is receiving cancer treatment, and she gave birth unexpectedly this morning.

We are going to go home on Sunday afternoon if you are well enough after the 48 hours of chemo. Our fingers are crossed...

Saturday 6 September 2014

It is your friend Ruby's 1st Birthday today, and we will soon be celebrating all your little friends' 1st Birthdays. Where has this year gone? What a year it has been. It wasn't supposed to turn out quite like this.

Just waiting for Daddy, Jack and Molly. They stayed in the house again last night, but I don't think they like being there without us. We are hoping to go out for a walk later, maybe up to Broomhill and have a coffee and cake in one of the coffee shops. It would be nice to try to do something normal with Jack and Molly. You are busy sleeping – no wonder you are tired, you have been up since 5am. I certainly feel tired.

We have just received an email from the Rector in Wingerworth.

Happy Days, Before You Were Ill

Above: Celebrating Mummy's birthday in May 2014 with her best friend Helen.

Above: Grandad Evison meets you for the first time in October 2013.

Above: Auntie Steph and you, just a couple of months before you became poorly.

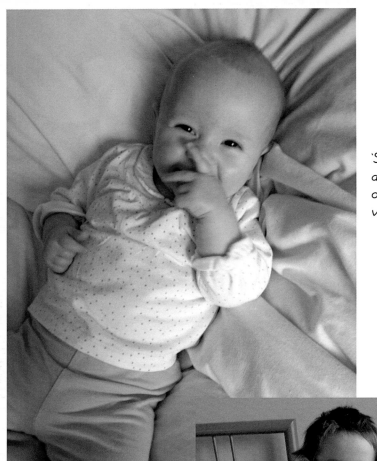

'Smiler'! One of Mummy's all-time favourite photos of you, taken when you were about 6 months old.

Jack and Molly meet their new baby sister for the first time.

Above: Emily, Lucy and Thomas in July 2014, when I first became concerned about how lethargic you were, just weeks before you were admitted into Chesterfield Royal Hospital.

Below: Mummy's best friends Jen (left) and Sonja (right) meet you for the first time.

Above: Lucy at the Waterbabies' class in May 2014.

Below: Ioan and Lucy. One of many playdates to come.

Before you became ill, having fun with one of your favourite toys.

With Auntie Selina, when you were just a few days old.

Hospital Days, Weeks, Months...

Sheffield Children's Hospital. This is the oldest part of the building, which is currently undergoing extensive refurbishment and improvement.

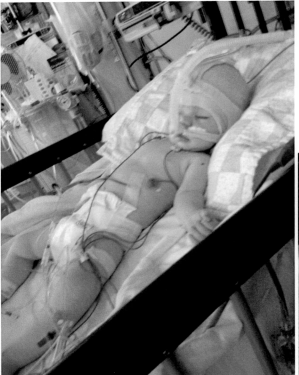

This is one of the first photographs I took of you following the first major operation. You had been in theatre since 8am and we finally arrived on the high dependency unit (HDU) at about 8pm.

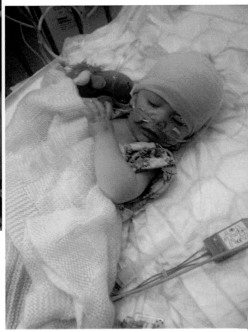

Snuggles with Cow Cow, your faithful companion to theatre.

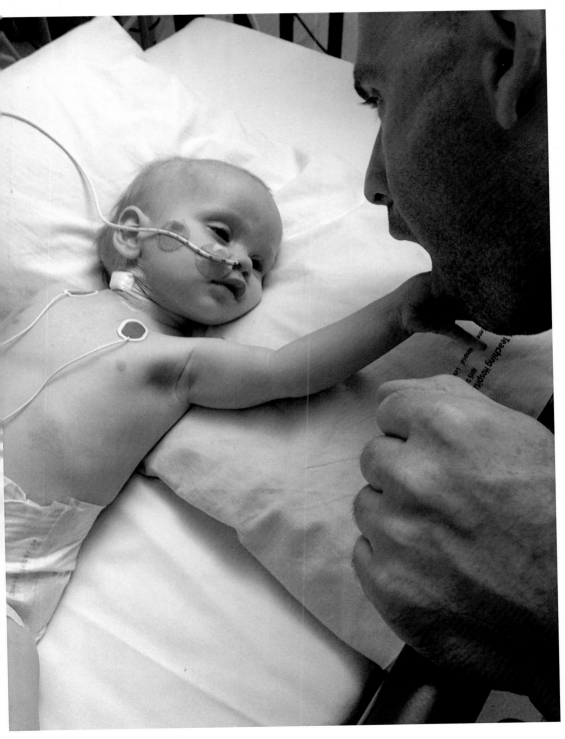

One of the first glimpses of you feeling a bit better following the first major operation.
You reached out to touch Daddy's nose.

After the first operation, a loving kiss from Mummy.

The Church Centre Manager must have told him about you being poorly when I emailed to cancel the birthday party. It was a very kind message. Although Daddy and I aren't religious, it is comforting to know people want to pray for us. People who don't even know us are wishing you well and sending messages of love and support.

The chemo started yesterday at 6.30pm so I don't think we'll be going home until Monday morning. I feel better about that, rather than rushing home. Daddy will take the day off on Monday, so the three of us can spend some time together – out of hospital.

Jack and Molly will be having their first day back at school after the summer holidays. Molly will be going into Year Two and Jack into Year Eight – they are growing up fast. Daddy and I are sad that their summer has been turned upside down, but they have been fantastic. Their summer holiday was cancelled and they've not seen Daddy as much as they normally would. The impact of all this on them is just immense, but they love you to bits and just want you better.

Watching you have the chemo is another surreal moment, with this bright red liquid being pumped into your tiny little body. It looks harmless and so innocent – but far from it. Your bottle of medicine is kept in a cute little ladybird bag, but it is a very strong drug (Doxorubicin), although hopefully one will that help to get rid of the last bit of the tumour. It is also the drug that will probably make you lose the lovely blonde hair that you have just started to grow. But hair can always grow back... can't it? Daddy seems to cope with very little, too!

You are coping really well with the chemo, better than Mummy, and still managing to tolerate all your other medicines and milk. You are such an amazing little girl. I will never forget how brave and strong you are, going through these very difficult times. Daddy and I are so very proud of you. I look forward to the day when I can sit down with you and tell you all about this horrible time; but we'll also look at all the lovely cards people have sent you, and the photos and videos that I have taken of you. Sometimes I fear that day may never come, but then I stop and remind myself to never stop believing. You will get better and this will just be a distant memory… xxx

Sunday 7 September 2014

Our friend Dave, Helen's husband, and Daddy to Ella and Isabel, is participating in the Great North Run today in Newcastle. He has been raising sponsorship money for The Sick Children's Trust and for Macmillan Cancer Support: charities that we never anticipated just a few weeks ago would mean so much to us. If anything good is to come out of this horrible time then it is raising money and awareness for these wonderful charities. We are so grateful to all our friends who are doing this. You seem to have inspired quite a few, Lucy.

I started to get ready to go home today. So exciting! I took down all the cards and pictures and packed our bags. I can't believe how much stuff we have here, although it has been our home for the last four weeks – the car will be full. You are still coping well with your first dose of chemo and not really showing any side effects. I hope this continues for as long as possible.

Back Home

✦

Briefly…

Monday 8 September 2014

Three exciting things are happening today:

★ It is Uncle Mark's birthday.

★ Auntie Sam is giving birth to her baby girl.

★ WE'RE GOING HOME!

We are thrilled to be taking you home, but it is very emotional too, as we walked into the house. I would never have imagined when we took you to the out-of-hours doctor at Chesterfield hospital late on that Saturday night that we wouldn't be home for four weeks, let alone all the stuff that has happened in between. Sometimes it all just feels like a bad dream. I really wish it was just that.

I don't think I've ever been away from my home as long as a month before. We were touched to see a lovely surprise from our neighbours Marjorie and David: a bottle of wine, some beer, a box of chocolates, a plant and a little toy duck for you. They are such very kind neighbours.

It was an unforgettable joy to put you to bed in your own house tonight. You looked so content and peaceful in your cot. We love you so much… xxx

Tuesday 9 September 2014

Today we went with Sian and Ioan on that much anticipated walk around Stubbing Court. It's a walk we used to do nearly every day together. I wore my Pandora bracelet from Sian, with the little duckling charm. It was very emotional, but a lovely morning. Sian was delighted to see us and have us home. We bumped into Sarah and Millie on the way back from our walk. Millie has grown so much and still absolutely gorgeous. It is a strange to think that one day, hopefully, the three of you will be in the same class at school.

Wednesday 10 September 2014

Another big surprise today – some beautiful flowers were delivered to our house from Sian, Sarah and Katie as a welcome home present. We are truly blessed to have such wonderful friends living nearby. They are still busy training for the Sheffield 10k Run, raising money for Treetops. They are all busy at home with their little ones, yet they are finding the time to do this. The total raised so far is already £850. It is amazing. It is about a month to go before the run. I'm making little goody bags and writing some Thank You cards for them today. It is not much, but I need to do something to show them how much I appreciate their efforts.

Thursday 11 September2014

Another day at home, enjoying the sunshine and going for walks around the village. The community nurse and the physiotherapist came to see you today. They were very pleased with the progress you are making since your major surgery.

Friday 12 September to Sunday 14 September

A whole weekend at home with Daddy, Jack and Molly. We've been looking forward to this for weeks, but now I have to start getting things ready for hospital tomorrow.

Monday 15 September 2014

We have returned to the hospital for a kidney test. It was supposed to be just a day visit but you were very sick last night and while we were at hospital this morning you were very unsettled and your temperature went up to 38 degrees, so they want to keep you in. It is disappointing because we had lots of visitors and things planned for Tuesday and Wednesday at home. But if you are unwell I would rather you are here so that everything is at hand should you need it.

Tuesday 16 September 2014

We are tired today after a sleepless night for both of us. We are not in a separate room this time, but in a bay with five other children and their parents. Everyone is friendly and supportive, but I would rather have our own space. It was noisy till late at night, but of course that is not anyone's fault. Children need different treatments and they are all on monitors which bleep regularly. I am fed up with the bleeps, and it's hard without Daddy here. The days seem really long.

Wednesday 17 September 2014

We both had a fairly good sleep last night and when you woke, you gave me a smile and a happy face. Daddy stayed at Treetops last night and came to see you before he went to work this morning. The antibiotics you were given have brought your temperature back to normal and your neutrophil count has gone back up – which is really good. It looks like you're back to your fighting self.

Neutrophils seem to be key to the whole treatment process. They are the most abundant type of white blood cell in our bodies and they form an essential part of our immune system. A fall in the neutrophil count makes you feel very poorly and susceptible to infection. Chemotherapy often reduces the number of neutrophils in your body and that's why you become poorly between treatment cycles – your body becomes run down and prone to infection. It also means if your body hasn't repaired itself by the time the next dose of chemotherapy is due, then it may have to be postponed until your neutrophil count has recovered.

'Neutrophils'

A neutrophil is a type of white blood cell; a type of immune cell that is one of the first cell types to travel to the site of an infection.

Neutrophils help fight infection by ingesting micro-organisms and releasing enzymes that kill the organisms.

Fingers crossed we should be able to go ahead with the second dose of chemo as planned. I never thought that would be something I would be wishing for. On the one hand I don't want you to have the chemo again, because it might make you poorly, but we've got to make sure we don't give the tumour any chance of coming back. You're going to win this fight, Lucy, I just know it.

Thursday 18 September 2014

After a night spent worrying about whether your neutrophil count was high enough to have the second round of chemotherapy, we finally got the go-ahead this morning. I took you and 'Cow Cow' to the operating theatre. It's a journey I hate and I will never, never get used to seeing you be put to sleep. I get so scared you might never wake up. The nurses and anaesthetists are always kind, reassuring and immensely patient with me. I hate walking out of the room once you have fallen to sleep and I come out in floods of tears every time.

You were only in theatre for 45 minutes before the buzzer went off (we had been given a pager to alert us to return to Recovery). You were fast asleep when I came to see you. You got really cranky when you did wake up. I don't blame you – I think I would be the same, or worse. You wanted to be cuddled and you held your arms up for me to pick you up. It was the best sight in the world and I happily obliged.

You are hooked up to your chemo drip and sleeping peacefully. I hope it doesn't make you feel too sick when you wake up, but you have been very sleepy since coming out of theatre. You slept pretty much all of last night, then had a two hour nap and now you are napping again. Something tells me you will be late to bed tonight.

It is Ioan's 1st Birthday on Saturday. I have bought a special 'friends' photo frame with a photo of you and him in it. It will soon be your 1st Birthday too – what an 'interesting' year it has been.

If this chemo goes well, we'll be home again by Sunday night or Monday morning.

Friday 19 September 2014

You were sick all over Daddy at 6am this morning, just as he was about to leave for work; then you were sick all over me this afternoon. It's the effects of the chemo. Poor you, I wish I could be sick for you. Despite feeling poorly, you have been managing to smile at the nurses and have been playing in your cot.

I have been busy working on something these last few weeks and I am now in full planning mode, with lists galore. By the time you are reading this I guess you will know that Mummy loves writing lists – Nannie and Auntie Claire tease me about it all the time.

The big news is that I have decided to organise a Charity Auction Night to raise money for all the charities that have been supporting us. It struck me one day that we should to do something to say 'thank you'. I also know it will keep me busy. I am used to having a busy job and not doing anything all day in here is driving me bonkers. Keeping busy also stops me from thinking about everything too much. The charities I want to support are:

★ The Children's Hospital Charity

★ The Sick Children's Trust (Treetops)

★ PACT (Parents and Children Together), which is M3's own charity and has funded all sorts of things, including the parent chair-beds

★ New Life, who provided you with a multisensory play pod

★ Read Well, who offer free books to children in hospital

★ Beads of Courage. You have been collecting a different bead for everything that has been happening. I can't wait to show you these when you are older.

We are going to have an Auction Night in January, probably at the Smithy Pond pub in Wingerworth. Our friends, Nicky and James, manage the pub. We already have our first donation for a raffle prize or an auction lot, a cake of your choice for any occasion, homemade by the fabulous cake maker herself, Tamara. There are other promises too, so we hope to have lots of donations. I think this was a good idea of Mummy's.

Saturday 20 and Sunday 21 September 2014

Another weekend here on M3. You are not very well because of the chemo. It is making you quite sick, with projectile vomiting in the playroom at 7.30am on Saturday, and you were very sleepy all day. Daddy and I enjoyed our cuddles with you but we hope you start to feel better soon.

Jack and Molly visited on Saturday and stayed in Treetops with Daddy. You smiled and giggled at them when they came to see you early on Sunday morning. We are so grateful that they are able to stay in Treetops with Daddy. I think it was a bit of a novelty for them and they were quite excited to stay. It is lovely up there, with double rooms and family rooms, a kitchen, a lounge area and even a playroom full of toys for siblings when they visit. It is a home from home for families to use at these very difficult times but is completely dependent on charity donations. It says on various posters around the hospital that it costs £28 per night per room to keep it open. I am pleased that Sian, Sarah and Katie are fundraising for them, and that is why we need to do the Charity Night. I've lost count of the number of nights Daddy has used Treetops. I don't know what we would have done without it.

It is nap time for you and so it is Mummy's time to email lots of companies. No time for 'Candy Crush' anymore. I've just had a response from a local artist saying she will donate a piece of her work. It's getting quite exciting.

We'll find out tomorrow whether we are able to go home…

Tuesday 23 September 2014

The hospital let us take you home but I'm not sure we'll be here for long. You are really not well and very, very sleepy. Evie and Kaz, our friends from Waterbabies, came to visit but you didn't really feel up to visitors. We'll see how tonight goes. My overnight bag is ready, just in case.

Wednesday 24 September 2014

You did not improve and after a sleepless night, we took you back to hospital, arriving just before midday. Nannie has come with us. She was coming on the train from Skegness to see you for the day at our house, so we picked her up from the train station and then headed straight here. We spent the day in the waiting room. Once you had been sick and your temperature reached 38 degrees, they decided to keep you in. Poor you and poor Nannie – not a good day, at all.

Thursday 25 September 2014

Today hasn't got much better. Your neutrophil count is worryingly low, as is your red blood cell count. You need a blood transfusion and some antibiotics. This is not how I wanted to spend the day before your 1st Birthday.

Your 1st Birthday

✦

Presents and Problems

Friday 26 September 2014

Today is your 1ˢᵗ Birthday! Happy Birthday to you, our gorgeous, brave little girl… xxx

Last night was probably the most upsetting for a while. I was very unhappy that you would be in hospital for your birthday and that I had nothing here to give you. Even though you probably wouldn't feel like opening your parcels and playing with presents, I wanted to do something, and I had such big plans for this special birthday.

So, late last night I drove back to the house. Thank goodness it was dark and no one could see me as I cried my eyes out all the way home. I've not left you in weeks and I hated going home without you. Why was I going home? I never imagined this would be how we would be preparing for your birthday. I should have making the sandwiches or putting the finishing touches to your friends party bags. Not this.

Back at the house, I picked up the cards and presents that people had sent you, before heading back to the hospital. I hastily wrapped some of the things that we bought you weeks ago. I'm pleased I did this, because it will be nice for you to have them on your special day. It will be a birthday to remember that's for sure.

This morning dawned and at 5am the nurses put up a birthday banner by your cot that they had made themselves – bless them all. I will to show you the photographs one day. They also gave you a present from them all. It's a musical wibbly wobbly toy thing. We are not sure what else to call it, but you love it anyway.

I decorated your bedside with your cards, and you had so many. Auntie Alison and Uncle Mark and Katie sent you a special birthday bear with two balloons. He is lovely. I hope you still have him when you read this, and have kept him safe over the years. Imogen and her mum Clair, in the bed opposite from us, bought you a pink balloon too, so your cot looked very colourful. Imogen is only five and she is receiving treatment for Leukaemia. Her mum is finding things difficult to deal with, just like me, so I was touched that she went to the trouble to buy something for you on your special day. I have a feeling the friends we make here will be friends for life. We have shared the worst times of our lives together; no one else will understand them.

Nannie bought you a musical toy dog, which made me smile as I was driving back from the house to the hospital last night. It kept going off in the boot, singing to me, scaring the living daylights out of me. I don't think Nannie found the 'off' button when she wrapped it up. Auntie Claire bought you a Talking Teapot with cups and cakes that you love playing with. Helen bought you some beautiful 'Lucy' bunting which I have hung on your cot (I wonder if you still have it now). Uncle James bought you some Lego blocks and Granny has knitted you a smart pink cardigan, and she also gave you a doll and some Duplo.

Daddy and I bought you a large wooden activity table. It is too big to bring to hospital, so we put it up in the living room, for you to see it as soon as you come home again. It wasn't the birthday we had planned, or the one we were ever expecting, but although you spent most of your birthday asleep, we hope we made it special for you. Happy 1st Birthday, Lucy. We love you so much… xxx

Saturday 27 September 2014

Jack and Molly stayed with Daddy at Treetops again last night and you smiled and wriggled when you saw them this morning. You are still quite poorly, being sick a few times a day and not really managing your milk. The doctors took you for an x-ray today, to check nothing is wrong with your tummy. We think it is just the chemo, but you are due another dose soon, so we need to get you better…

Grandad Geoff, Nanna Kaz, Steph and Selina visited today. They bought you lots of lovely presents. You have been awake most of the day.

Sunday 28 September 2014

You are very sleepy and a bit grumpy. Your neutrophils, red blood cells and platelets are all really low and making you very poorly, bless you. We are hoping the levels will improve but you might need a bit of help. I don't think you'll be having your next dose of chemo tomorrow. It will probably be on Thursday.

We are waiting for Auntie Alison and Uncle Mark to arrive. I wonder if they'll bring you more birthday presents? Auntie Alison does like to spoil you.

Monday 29 September 2015

You are starting to lose your hair now. It is much thinner and there are patches where hair has rubbed off altogether. Maybe you just want to be like Daddy.

Auntie Alison has bought you a lovely winter hat and matching cardigan. They will be perfect for our winter walks when we are home.

You were due to start your third dose of chemo today but you are not yet strong enough. We will wait until Thursday, or it might be next Monday. I wonder whether we'll manage to go home? You are still having some fluids through a drip, although you have just had your first proper milk feed again, so fingers crossed that you on are the up. He first time in ages, you weren't sick last night, so that is progress too.

Think you will be weighed today. Last Monday you were 15 lbs – tiny for a one-year-old. It makes me feel so very sad, as you were a good weight when you were born, 8 lbs 9½ oz. You were doing well with weaning at 10 months old before all this happened. I think you might have lost a bit of weight this week, with all the sickness and several days on just maintenance fluids. No wonder you've had no energy. My poor little poppet.

I am still busy planning the charity auction night, which will now be on Saturday 24 January at Smithy Pond. My job today is to be on the scrounge for someone to print the raffle tickets for free.

Home Again

✦

Lucy in the News

Wednesday 1 October 2014

We came home yesterday! With luck, we won't be heading back to hospital until next Monday.

I had a lovely day at home today and you played with all your birthday toys. Other than a runny nose you seem really well, which is heartening to see. Lots of smiles and giggles... you are amazing.

Nannie has got the fundraising bug. I think it distracts us all from what we are facing, and you inspire us all. She is planning a Halloween Coffee Morning to raise some money for The Sick Children's Trust. It will be at her workplace, Aspen Lodge in Skegness. I am pleased some good can come out of all this.

Thursday 2 October 2014

Something very exciting happened yesterday. You were on the front page of *The Derbyshire Times*. I have kept you a copy. I say exciting, but I don't know if that's the best way to describe how I felt. I felt really tearful when I first caught sight of it in the shop earlier today. It's not that I want everyone to read about your suffering either, the idea behind it was to publicise the auction and hopefully generate more interest in it. I do hope you'll understand this one day and not be cross at me for plastering you all over the local paper.

I didn't know it was going to be in this week's issue, let alone on the front page. I must admit, I always thought your first appearance in the local paper might be similar to my first time, which were playgroup pictures or singing at a care home with the Brownies or something like that. But this is very different – front page news!

It is a gorgeous picture of you, albeit in your head bandage, and you look so smiley and brave. You are cuddling the special Tigger toy that Granny bought for you after your first operation. I feel so incredibly proud of you. Seeing the newspaper in the shop took me by surprise and I began to cry. A little old lady saw me, just one look at you in the pushchair and then at the newspaper article and said, 'Oh, is that your little girl on the front page?' 'Bless you dear' and squeezed my hand. That made me cry even more, so I grabbed ten copies, hurriedly paid for them and got our the shop as quickly as possible.

I bought ten copies because I knew Nannie and Auntie Claire and probably a few other people would like a copy. I was still sniffling all the way home. You probably wondered what all the fuss was about.

The article certainly did the trick, and I have already had a few incredibly kind people ring me offering donations. One caller was a 93-year-old lady called Mrs Evans, who had cancer when she was 83. She told me that she wants to donate a piece of equipment 'that helps circulation'. I don't know what it is, but how kind of her. I will pick it up from her in a few days' time.

Then a lady called Danielle sent me a text. She lives in Hasland and has terminal ovarian cancer herself. She is just 28 and has two young boys aged 6 and 8. It is so very sad. Yet she still wants to help you. How incredible is that? She just said she wanted to bring you a present and a donation for the auction. She came to the house that afternoon, carrying not just one present, but arms full of presents. She explained that they were from her and her best friend, Jane, who sadly lost two of her babies. They also bought £20 of Boots vouchers for the raffle on the auction night. Their kindness and generosity quite overwhelmed me, and there were many more tears. I have just sent them a thank you card from us, and would like to keep in touch with them.

Jack and Molly came home from school and you were full of smiles for them. We all had tea together, which was lovely and so nice to just do 'normal' things. You then decided to stay up till 10pm, you tinker! And you were awake again at 3am for more cuddles. Yawn…

Friday 3 October 2014

Another day at home today, just you and me. The nurse will be coming round shortly to take your blood. If your white blood cells and platelets are high enough you will be having your next dose of chemo on Monday and will probably be in hospital for a few days again. However, we hope to be home by the weekend, as some very special people are visiting – Helen, Jen and Sonja, my best friends from school. We all went to 'Skeggy' Grammar and they are my oldest and dearest best friends. They can't wait to see you. I also have a much needed hairdresser's appointment Saturday morning. So we must be home for all of that.

Saturday 4 October 2014

Jack and Molly went to the CLIC Sargent 'Sibling Day' today at the hospital. They seemed to have had a good time, joining some other brothers and sisters of children being treated for cancer at the hospital. The group talked about what cancer is and how it made them feel. They each made a sand glass ornament where all the different colours of the sand represented their feelings. Jack and Molly have placed theirs proudly in their bedrooms. I'm sure they will still have them when you are old enough to read this. I hope so. The nurses showed the children how they do a thumb prick, which you have done to you most days you are in hospital, when the nurses have to take your blood for testing. The group also visited the PACT house, to see where some of their families might stay, just like Daddy has done in recent weeks. I hope Jack and Molly found it helpful, even just a little.

Monday 6 October 2014

Back to hospital today for our regular appointment at the Oncology clinic, and to start your third dose of chemotherapy. It is weird that all this suddenly feels quite normal. Your treatment requires you to stay just one night and then we can go home tomorrow afternoon.

Wednesday 8 October 2014

Well Lucy, guess what happened today…

At 7.15am Mummy went on the local radio! It was Peak FM and I was interviewed by Becky Measures to promote the charity auction. They are calling you 'One of North East Derbyshire's Superstars'. The auction event has suddenly become a lot more exciting. It will now be held at the Proact Football Stadium in Chesterfield, thanks to Bernie Clifton (you won't have a clue who he is, but when I was young we children knew him as the funny man on the television, who had a famous toy stage prop, who misbehaved all the time. It was a bright yellow ostrich called 'Oswald', which Bernie 'rode' like a horse. He was a celebrity in his time, but now lives in the Peak District. He rang me last Thursday, after reading your article in *The Derbyshire Times*, asking if we would like him to be involved. Nannie thinks it's hilarious. I am going to meet him and someone from the football ground on Friday morning to make some plans. The thought makes a bit nervous, because I've not met anyone famous before.

More Tests

✦

More Treatment

Thursday 9 October 2014

Today we went to hospital, unusually just for the day. We normally have to stay over. You had to have a lumbar puncture and intrathecal drugs that you have every 2 weeks or so.

'Lumbar Puncture'

Inserting a hollow needle between two of the spinal bones to take a sample of cerebrospinal fluid (CSF), the fluid that surrounds and protects the brain and the spinal cord, or to inject chemotherapy (called 'intrathecal administation').

Thankfully you are put to sleep because you have to be very still while they do the injection. This time, you weren't asleep very long, just enough time for me to have a coffee in the hospital café before the pager starts to buzz. I hate that buzzing noise. It reminds me of your very first operation, but it also means that you are waking up, and that's good. You gave me a big surprise when I walked into the recovery room. You were wide awake, sitting up on the trolley bed, smiling and waving at all the other children and nurses. They were all laughing at you and saying how cute you are. Well of course – we've known that for ages.

I am sitting at home, waiting for Daddy to bring Jack and Molly from school. They are going to love pudding at tea time today. Tamara, my friend from work, has sent us a cake in the post. She bakes delicious cakes. She sends me messages every day since you were first diagnosed, so caring and thoughtful. She often tells me what cakes she is making that evening and always has lots of orders. I just happened to say, jokingly, 'I need some cake to help me get this charity night planned', and she arranged for a cake to be delivered in the post. It was a lovely surprise when it arrived. I think it is intended to cheer me up, to stay positive and to get through the sad days.

It's scary not knowing what is going to happen. The tumour you have is very fast growing and many children under three years old don't survive. Even with treatment the tumour commonly returns, and that's what terrifies me. Your high dose of chemotherapy in December will be the last – your tiny body just wouldn't be to cope with more. You are too young for radiotherapy, so the chemo you are having now, plus the high dose chemo and stem cell transplant that you will have in December just has to work. We've had a letter today informing us of your first MRI scan – the first scan since starting your chemotherapy. The little bit that was left over after the main surgery may well still be there, but as long as it hasn't grown and there are no signs of other tumours...

Monday 20th October is scan day. That seems an awful long way away. Thankfully I have the auction night plan to keep me busy – one of the main reasons for doing it.

Friday 10 October

It is a big day today. I am meeting Bernie Clifton! There's a statement I never thought I would write.

Saturday 11 October 2014

Bernie was charming and the meeting went well. The auction has suddenly become a much bigger event, with potentially 200 people attending. Chesterfield Football Club have offered to print the tickets for us free of charge, in the same format as their football tickets. They have also offered a DJ for the night and balloons for every table, in colours of our choice. We will have a 'pie and pea' supper, to be followed by the auction and the raffle. I hope I haven't I bitten off more than I can chew. I hope not, and I hope that one day you'll be proud of Mummy and Daddy for what they tried to do. We want to use the event to say 'Thank You' to all the wonderful charities that have supported us. I'm sure we can pull it off.

Helen, Sonja and Jen visited today. Helen bought you a bag of clothes that Izzy and Ella have grown out of. Sonja bought us a bag of goodies with something for everyone in it – beer for Daddy, Wine for Mummy, sweets and biscuits for Jack and Molly and a cute little hedgehog toy called 'Chester' (because we live in Chesterfield.). Jen brought two beautiful bunches of flowers. The four of us have been best friends since secondary school. They were terribly upset about your illness have been such good friends to me. I hope that one day you make special friends like these.

The four of us went for an excellent Italian meal at 'Viva' in Matlock. It is where Mummy and Daddy went for their fourth anniversary in June. I should tell you that I felt quite brave leaving you with Daddy. Not brave because I left you with Daddy, he's a wonderful Daddy to you, but brave because I find it very difficult to leave you.

A Turn for the Worse

✦

And We Discover G-CSF

Monday 13 October 2014

Things took a turn for the worse overnight and this morning your temperature went up to 38.6 degrees. Daddy and I are taking you to hospital a bit earlier than planned. Daddy has phoned his work to say he won't be in today – you are more important and you really do seem poorly. I didn't want to take you back to hospital on my own.

We were soon on M3 ward, where they decided to give you some blood and fluids, antibiotics and some stronger anti-sickness drugs. You are very sleepy now. Let's hope you perk up tomorrow. I hate seeing you like this.

Tuesday 14 October 2014

You slept quite well last night and seemed a bit brighter this morning. You should be well enough to have your chemo later. Maybe we'll be home again tomorrow. It's amazing how quickly you recover. What a strong little lady you are, not like Mummy, who complains at the slightest headache.

Thursday 16 October 2014

We were back at home yesterday by about 5pm, but you are very poorly again today. We're not sure what's happened. You've been sick three times and your temperature is creeping up to 38 degrees again. If it gets that high we have to go back to hospital, because you have low levels of white blood cells and there is a chance you have an infection. The doctors call it being 'neutropenic'.

There's some treatment for that… it's amazing how every problem that you encounter seems to be treatable, but with uncertain results.

Friday 17 October 2014

You seem a lot better today and unusually sleeping in till 9am. You were having cuddles on Daddy's tummy from 3.45 to 5am – you do love your Daddy.

The nurse has been to the house to give you some G-CSF to help boost your neutrophils. We hope that this will make it possible for you to have your chemo on Monday, but I expect you'll probably need a few more days of the G-CSF treatment. They inject it over about half an hour through your Portacath and you don't even notice you are having it. Medicine is just amazing. I have learnt so much these last few weeks... but I wish I didn't have to know about such things.

'Neutropenia' and 'G-CSF'

Having chemotherapy can affect the bone marrow, reducing its ability to make white blood cells, a condition called neutropenia that can increase the risk of infection.

G-CSF (granulocyte-colony stimulating factor) is a type of protein called a growth factor.

It stimulates the bone marrow to make white blood cells.

Sunday 19 October 2014

Today was a very special and sometimes an emotional day. Our friends, Sian, Katie and Sarah completed the Sheffield 10k Run at Endcliffe Park, in Sheffield. They have raised well over £1000 for the Sick Children's Trust (which funds Treetops). I was quite tearful (again) watching them hold hands to cross the finish line. It was even more special because you were there with me. A few days ago I worried that you might not be well enough to come out to watch, but you were there, waving and clapping at our kind, generous friends.

Monday 20 October 2014

We went to hospital today for your MRI scan. I felt sick, couldn't eat, didn't sleep, and felt tearful all day. We won't get the results till Thursday but have to back at the hospital tomorrow for your chemo treatment. There were no beds available on M3 ward today. We are going to go back and collect the chemo tomorrow and administer it at home. It is the one in the ladybird bag again so once the nurses have set it up we can then come home with it attached to you.

Tuesday 21 October

It was practically a hurricane out there today and we both got soaked getting out the car and into hospital. We are safely home now, with the ladybird bag next to you. You are very sleepy today and full of cold. We can be at home until Thursday when we return to the hospital for a lumbar puncture in theatre and for the MRI scan results. Daddy will be with us on Thursday so he is there for the results.

Wednesday 22 October 2014

You are very poorly today, sleeping until 9am, but you had been wide awake during the night, coughing non-stop from 1 to 3am. You are still full of cold with a delightful green snotty nose.

The chemo doesn't seem to be bothering you yet. It takes a few days to hit you and for your neutrophil levels to drop, and then you get poorly. It is horrible waiting and just knowing that's how you will feel soon.

Thursday 23 October 2014

Oh Happy Day! We had positive news from the scan results. The bit that remained after surgery is still there but it has not grown, nor become worse in any way. This should mean that the chemo is working. You have only had one chemo cycle, so with two more rounds to go, plus the high dose chemo, there is every chance that it may disappear. However, the doctors explained that the MRI scan cannot deliver precise results. The mass that was revealed on this occasion could be the remains of the tumour, as intended, or it might be scar tissue from the operation, or just dead matter. They don't know and that is especially hard for Daddy and me to cope with. But let's focus on today's good news: there will be another scan in six weeks.

In the meantime, I need to plan our early Christmas Day. Because the high chemo dose and the stem cell transplant is planned to be done over Christmas, we want to celebrate our family Christmas before you go into hospital.

I have had confirmation from Chesterfield Football Club that we can hold the Charity Auction at their Proact Stadium on Friday 30th January. The donation keep coming in: a Waterbabies swimming course, a soft play party (donated by Chuckle Chimps, who were going to do Lucy's 1st Birthday party), a voucher from Wings Photography, loads of vouchers from hairdresser and beauty salons, wine, chocolates, champagne and plenty more.

Saturday 25 and Sunday 26 October 2014

You were quite poorly yesterday, so we had a quiet day at home. It was just Molly with us as Jack is camping with the Scouts on something called the 'Chilly Challenge' – very well-named for the weather this week.

You are being sick a couple of times a day and are very sleepy. Poor little poppet. It's probably the chemotherapy. You have been lucky so far, but maybe the last cycle is producing these side-effects.

We have learned that one of Daddy's ex-colleagues, Steve Miller, is planning a 'cabaret night' to raise funds for the Sheffield Children's Hospital Charity. He has become my new Facebook friend and although I have never met him, I'm delighted that he is helping to fundraise for the hospital. I don't think that both Daddy and I will be able to attend the event, but one of us will go show our support.

A colleague of mine, Rachel Sykes, will be running the Leicester Half Marathon and has chosen CLIC Sargent as her chosen charity. Daddy and I are honoured that so many friends and colleagues have been inspired by your story to raise money for charity.

Monday 27 October 2014

Back to hospital today for a regular check: a blood test and to have your height and weight measured.

Tuesday 28 October 2014

It is your cousin Thomas's third birthday today. The last time we saw him, with his sister Emily and Auntie Claire and Uncle Ben was at the beginning of July, when they stayed in a caravan in Skegness for the week, visiting Nannie and Grandad. There is an adorable photograph of you in the caravan, sitting on Emily's knee and sucking your thumb. You used to love sucking your thumb but it's something you don't do anymore. Looking more closely at the picture, you seem to be very sleepy and I wonder now if that's when you started to feel poorly. It is horrible to think that the tumour had perhaps started growing by the time this photo was taken.

In and Out of Hospital

✦

Whilst Fundraising Plans Go Well

Wednesday 29 October 2014

You slept all day yesterday and when we got to hospital today for a kidney test, your temperature had spiked and you were sickly and sleepy. I hate days like this when I feel so helpless.

We are staying in the hospital for 48 hours. You will have fluids, antibiotics, a continuous feed at night and some G-CSF to give your neutrophils a boost. All that, before starting the next lot of chemo on Monday.

Thursday 30 October 2014

Daddy was able to have a room at Treetops last night, which was great as it meant he could stay with us till late last night and see you before he went to work this morning. You woke up much happier today and played with Daddy before he went to work – all before 6.30am. I'm not looking forward to another long day in hospital, but it has to be.

We had some fantastic news yesterday about a prize for the Charity Auction and Raffle. I emailed all the holiday companies we have ever used and one of them, a company called holidaycottages.co.uk, replied with an offer of a £500 voucher to use on any of their cottages. That's an amazing offer and we will make it the First Prize in our raffle. It should help to sell more tickets.

I can't believe how generous they are being, but there is more! They also want to offer us a free holiday for our family at the company owner's cottage in the Cotswolds when you are a bit better. That is something for the five of us to look forward to in the New Year. You should be feeling better by then, and all your treatment has finished. Wow! Thank you holidaycottages.co.uk.

Friday 31 October

It is Halloween. The ward is decorated and it looks appropriately spooky.

We are going to go home today; just for the weekend but it will be good for you to spend it with Jack and Molly. You love being with them.

Sunday 2 November 2014

It is difficult to believe that it's November. It was a warm 20 degrees yesterday. We enjoyed our day at home Jack and Molly. Granny and Uncle James came round for Sunday dinner. In the afternoon, while Granny played with you, I went into town to donate blood. It was at the Proact Stadium where the auction will be held. I donated blood once when I was 18 and I have never managed to do so again since then. However, after seeing you have four or five blood transfusions already, it made me realise that it is really important thing to do; and so simple. The next session is in February so I have booked that one too. Daddy feels frustrated he can't do it because he had a blood transfusion when he had a big operation on his lungs. Apparently if you have received donated blood you then can't donate yourself.

Monday 3 November 2014

Back at hospital today for check-up clinic appointment and then up to the ward for chemo. You have actually gained some weight for the first time in weeks. We are so pleased. You now weigh 6.5kg. This is still very small for a thirteen-month-old girl.

Once on the ward you were sick after your 3pm milk. I thought that odd, because you had been well all weekend. It is too soon for the effects of chemo to start, so I'm worried that it might be the start of another infection. You haven't got a temperature, which is unusual, it normally goes up at times like this. They have taken some samples, so we'll see if they come up with any answers.

Wednesday 5 November 2014

Bonfire Night, but you are too poorly this year to go out to watch any fireworks. We will make sure we celebrate it next year.

You are sleeping a great deal today, giving me some time for me to catch up with online Christmas shopping. Because you are scheduled to be in hospital for a month from Monday 8th December, we have decided that our family will have Christmas Day on Sunday 7th December.

Thursday 6 November 2014

You are having a lumbar puncture in theatre today. When you have recovered form anaesthetic and your hydration has finished, we hope to be able to go home. We'll be home until the 17th. I don't think we've ever been at home for that long. I wonder if we'll manage it?

Friday 7 November 2014

Home again and you celebrated by staying in your cot until 7.30am. You did have me and Daddy up from 4 to 5.15am, but 'Thank You' poppet!

We've just been to the football ground to pick up the Charity Night tickets – it's getting very exciting. And I have finished this notebook; I must order another one so I can continue with the diary for you.

Saturday 8 November 2014

Waking up at home with Jack, Molly and Daddy is the best feeling. It is a miserable day out there today but you are having lots of fun with Jack and Molly and lots of smiles and giggles playing with your toys. You are still really well at the moment and the chemo has not stated to affect you. We have said that before though, haven't we?

Sunday 9 November 2014

There is lovely sunshine today, so different from yesterday. You, Molly and I went for a walk while Daddy and Jack went to the Poppy Parade for Remembrance Sunday.

You have begun to feel poorly this afternoon. I wonder if we'll end up back in hospital soon?

Monday 10 November 2014

Here we are, back in hospital, as predicted. You have a temperature and you have started to be quite sick. The community nurse had to come out in the middle of the night (again) to replace your feeding tube. The hospital has put you on a 48-hour infusion of antibiotics. With luck we will be here only until Wednesday.

Wednesday 12 November 2014

You started to perk up a bit yesterday and you were smiling at all the doctors and nurses. It was good that we came back to hospital on Monday. You have needed antibiotics, fluids, a blood transfusion and some potassium on a drip – the full works.

A friend brought me coffee and breakfast up to the ward. Such simple things are all I need to keep me smiling.

Thursday 13 November 2014

We came home last night but it was a dreadful night. You were up nearly every hour; hot and grizzly all night. The community nurse came out this morning and replaced your feeding tube again. It comes out when you are sick or wretch. I have lost count the number of tubes you have had reinserted and you hate it. I absolutely hate having to watch it happen to you. We both usually end up in tears. I have so much respect and admiration for the nurses. The community nurse said this morning that we should probably go back to Sheffield because of your high temperature… so that's where we are now.

Friday 14 November 2014

You had a platelet infusion and some fluids and we are now home again. It is amazing how quickly you get poorly and then recover. The doctors are very clever, but you are also made of tough stuff.

It is 'Children in Need' on TV tonight. I always

'Platelet Infusion'

Platelets are tiny cells in your blood which form clots to help stop bleeding.

Cancer and some cancer treatments can affect the bone marrow where platelets are made.

When this happens, the number of platelets in the blood becomes lower.

If the platelet count is too low, a platelet transfusion will be given, using platelets collected from blood donors.

watch and donate something. It is a strange emotion to think this year we could be one of the families in those sad video clips. I always cry. I'm going to find it hard to watch this year.

Saturday 15 November 2014

Auntie Alison, Uncle Mark and Katie came to visit today. We did our usual Christmas present swap, which seems very early this year, but then our family Christmas Day is only three weeks away. Jack and Molly have had fun playing with Katie on the Wii and you enjoyed playing with Uncle Mark, who makes you giggle so much.

Daddy had some bad news yesterday. The management at the company that he works for, in the job that he had only just started when you were diagnosed, have become impatient with all the time he has taken off to be with you. We don't think that it has been excessive, but because the first three months of a new job are classed as a probation period they have decided to not offer him a permanent contract and so, in effect, he has lost his job.

Three weeks before our Christmas Day… it seems very heartless. I must admit I lost my temper and phoned his boss. I know that it didn't achieve anything but it made me feel a little bit better, giving him a piece of my mind. I don't know what we are going to do. As if we haven't enough to worry about with the high dose treatment and stem cell transplant coming up. We are in shock. Daddy has never lost a job in his life, so he is very upset.

Sunday 16 November 2014

Something very special has happened today. You have managed to eat all by yourself – whilst on a break from the feeding tube, as you pulled it out earlier this morning. This is the first time you've attempted to eat something since August. It was only a few carrot stick crisp things and a little bit of toast, but it still brought a tear to Mummy's eyes. I'm so proud of you…

Monday 17 November 2014

We are back on the ward and you are about to start your next dose of chemo. You are especially happy today. I think you are trying to cheer up Mummy and Daddy. You babbled away at Vicki the consultant during our clinic appointment. She was delighted to see you looking well. It's only a 24-hour chemo treatment, so we hope to be home late tomorrow evening.

Tuesday 18 November 2014

You are happy and playful and we are on track to go home later today. My heart melts watching you and I am so very proud of you. I am looking forward to a day at home with just you and Daddy. It is nice having Daddy at home but hard to enjoy the time when we know why he's not at work. You are well and I am poorly at the moment, full of cold. Typical!

Some friends and colleagues at my workplace in Scunthorpe are busy hosting a charity event today to raise money for the same charities that we will be supporting at our own charity night. Their event has been organised by Donna Watson, the manager of the Learning Development Centre in Scunthorpe. She has offered me huge support since you were diagnosed. She sends messages frequently and always asks how you are getting on.

There will be a cake stall and a raffle, amongst other things. Donna sent me a copy of the PowerPoint presentation that she will have on display on the day, and that brought me to tears again. So much crying, but how else to respond to such generosity? You have inspired yet another person to raise funds for the wonderful charities supporting us.

We are due back at hospital on Thursday for your fortnightly lumbar puncture. Watching you being put to sleep never gets any easier. 'Cow cow' comes with you every time.

Friday 21 November 2014

Donna emailed me today to say that the charity event raised a massive £930.50. In addition, some people have placed cake orders, which will be added to make the final total. I am delighted and so grateful for their efforts.

My job involves working closely with the Speech and Language

Team in North Lincolnshire, and they have also been raising money. Together with some of the Occupational Therapists and the Physiotherapy Team, they have raised £130 from a cake sale. That represents a lot of cakes. I am overwhelmed by others' kindness. Times like this really do bring the best out in people.

The raffle tickets for the auction have arrived and I am busy putting all of them into envelopes, ready for people to sell. We are aiming to sell 3000 tickets; a challenging target but I'm sure we will manage it.

I am beginning to make plans for another charity event once this one is over. There are now more charities that we would like to support; especially those that will possibly help us with financial support while Daddy is out of work. They are Levi's Star, Ellie's Fund and Macmillan. We are very grateful to them and to our social worker, Pat, from CLIC Sargent, who has arranged it all. We haven't included these charities amongst those we are supporting this time, as we already have eight. So, we will just have to have a second charity night.

We would also like to support Amy's Retreat, as this is the charity, through CLIC Sargent, that has offered us a weekend away at Center Parcs, Sherwood Forest. We are hoping to take up the offer in February or March next year when your chemotherapy has finished and you should be feeling a bit better. That seems like a lifetime away...

Saturday 22 November 2014

We arrived home last night to another lovely surprise from our super neighbours. Marjorie and David prepared a scrumptious homemade pie for us, and some buns that Molly devoured.

You are still well at the moment but I wonder if you will start to dip soon. You usually do, a few days after you have had your chemotherapy. Daddy and I have planned a rare night out. He bought me tickets for my birthday, back in May, to see a comedian called John Bishop, at the Sheffield Arena. I hope we get to go, but I know I won't want to leave you if you are poorly.

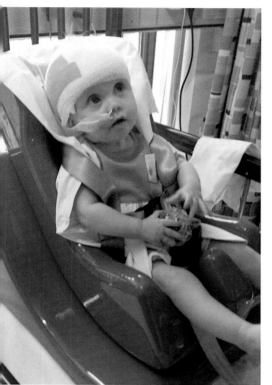

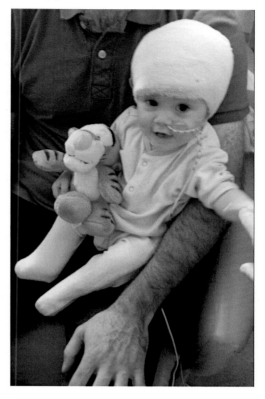

Surprising the nurses with your speedy recovery after anaesthetic.

Above: Jack and Molly came to visit you for the first time since you had been admitted into hospital. They had missed you terribly.

Below: The wonderful M3 nurses decorated your cot at 5am on your birthday morning on 26 September 2014 to help make the day as special as possible.

Derbyshire TIMES

CUTE KIDS 2014

VOTE NOW! Don't miss the chance to vote for your favourite

TURN TO PAGE **32**

Plucky pensioner plummets to Earth

PAGE **16**

TODDLER BATTLES BRAIN CANCER

FAMILY PLAN EARLY CHRISTMAS FOR BRAVE TOT

End
for C

BY DAN HOBSON
comment@derbyshiretimes.co.uk
@_DanHobson

A mum has spoken of her devastation after medics revealed her baby's illness was not due to a milk allergy as first thought – but a rare and aggressive brain cancer.

When baby Lucy, now one, started suffering from severe vomiting in July, mum Tracey Evison took her straight to Chesterfield Royal Hospital, where doctors suspected she might have a cows milk allergy.

But when her condition didn't improve after a few weeks worried Tracey, of Joseph Fletcher Drive, Wing-

erworth, took her daughter to an out-of-hours surgery and medics gave the tot a CT scan, which revealed a growth in her brain. Lucy was immediately rushed to Sheffield Children's Hospital for surgery – and underwent a gruelling 12-hour operation to remove as much of the growth as possible.

After the operation, brave

Lucy underwent an MRI scan.

But the results proved to be heartbreaking for parents Tracey, 34, and her 37-year-old partner Paul Needham – as doctors revealed Lucy had an extremely rare form of brain cancer, which she might not survive.

TURN TO PAGE 9 →

●● Mourner
the Dowager
passed away
The ceremo
Endsor, on
tributes ha
ager Duch
spects to a
worth. Se
derbyshi

You were front page news in the local press. Mummy contacted the Derbyshire Times to gain some publicity for the Charity Night. The newspaper people were very keen to hear about your story.

Daddy cuddles – one of the best medicines you could have whilst on high dose chemo.

A kiss in the park. This was taken on your first trip out of hospital in September 2014. You had not been outside for almost a whole month.

The high dose chemo left you feeling extremely tired.

Our dear friends, Sian, Katie and Sarah ran the Sheffield 10k and raised over £1000 in sponsorship for The Sick Children's Trust and Macmillan.

Celebrating our 'early' Christmas Day on 7 December 2014. The next day you would be heading off to hospital for a five week stay.

Above: Nannie Evison and Auntie Alison helping at the Charity Auction. On the night the helpers wore the bright yellow T-shirts from Sheffield Children's Hospital Charity.

Below: Uncle Mark and Daddy getting into the spirit of things at the Charity Auction.

Auntie Claire and Cousin Debs were excellent auction spotters on the night of the Charity Auction.

Uncle Ben and your big brother Jack having a boogie!

Clinics and Crises

✦

Family Plans are Changing

Sunday 23 November 2014

Daddy and I managed to go out for the evening. Granny came to look after you. You were sick late yesterday afternoon and we nearly changed our mind about going to the show. However, you slept all the way through and didn't wake once for Granny. I think she was looking forward to some cuddles. You woke up when we got home, though.

We are due back at the Oncology clinic tomorrow for a check-up. I'll bet we'll end up staying in…

Monday 24 November 2014

As predicted, here we are at hospital and staying in for at least 48 hours. You were very unsettled last night and your temperature spiked this morning. Blood tests show you need another blood platelets transfusion, some antibiotics and possibly some G-CSF later in the week. I sound like a nurse with all these medical words. We have had to learn so much since August – things that had not entered my world until then, nor would I have wished them to do so.

Daddy is here with me. He is still looking hard for a new job. For the first time since we came to the hospital, he couldn't get a room at Treetops last night. He stayed instead at the PACT house, which is just up the road. PACT is on our list for the charity night.

Tuesday 25 November 2014

Oh, I am so tired today. You were awake from midnight till 4am, and at 3am you were sick and the feeding tube came out. It was good that Daddy was able to come from the PACT house at 7am to play with you for a bit, while I tried to snooze. I didn't manage to sleep because it was noisy on the ward, and also because I like to be awake when the doctors come on their rounds. If all goes well, we'll be in our own beds tomorrow.

You had a lovely surprise on the ward today from the 'Giggle Doctors'. They certainly made you giggle and it was a pleasure to watch. 'Dr Bungee', as he called himself, made you an animal balloon and just generally tried to make you smile. It made me feel quite tearful watching your reaction and to see the amazing impact that yet another charity can have. This charity is called Theodora Children's Charity. They visit all the children's hospitals in the UK, dressing up in silly doctor clothes and spending lots of time with the children, with the intention of making poorly children a little happier. The Children's Hospital Charity supports them with funding. That is another good reason for supporting them at our charity night in January.

Wednesday 26 November 2014

It was another sleepless night for both of us. You seemed very poorly this morning but you have perked up this afternoon. You are having G-CSF and another platelet transfusion. We are still planning on going home.

I sat to watch a film this afternoon, which is a very rare thing for me to do. It was the Disney film 'Frozen' which everyone is raving about. I enjoyed it and the songs are now stuck in my head. I shall have to watch it with you one day.

Thursday 27 November 2014

We came home yesterday as planned, a bit poorly but hopefully on the mend. You were very excited to see Jack and Molly when they came home after school.

We came home to a lovely surprise too. A lady who lives in Wingerworth has read about us in the *Twist* magazine and she rang me to ask if she could donate a prize for the raffle – two bottles of champagne. They will make a fantastic raffle prize. The auction is really coming together now. I have posted out 114 auction tickets so far and there are more to do before you wake up from your nap....

Friday 28 November 2014

Another miserable rainy day and I expect we'll be indoors again for most of it. You are much better this morning, bouncing up and down on our bed at 6.30am.

Daddy has just taken Jack and Molly to school and then he is going to go and see his old work colleagues in Sheffield. I think he now wishes that he had not left there in the summer, but he would have been working abroad, which would have been impossible for the family, And so he had to leave. Many of his ex-colleagues are coming to the auction and have bought lots of raffle tickets, which is very kind of them.

Jenny, the health visitor who first sent us off to the doctors at the end of July, will be calling at our house today. She delivers my doctor's 'sick note' for me; another three-month note that takes me until the end of February. I really wish I knew when I can go back to work but I must not that about that yet. My attention is focused on you and getting you better. I can't see how I'll be ready to return to work in March. You will almost certainly still have the feeding tube and possibly also have a PEG tube fitted, which means another stay in hospital. The PEG will be easier than having the NG tubes, which are not ideal for long term use. The NG tube comes out quite often and has to be re-inserted. That's very distressing for you. You are not gaining much weight and so we have a long way to go still. I don't think I could focus on work just yet.

Doesn't matter how small the steps are, just keep taking them.

Saturday 29 November 2014

It's time for Daddy to get the Christmas Tree and decorations down from the loft, ready for our early Christmas Day next Sunday. Jack and Molly are going to a Christmas Party today, organised by CLIC Sargent at the hospital – bowling and then out for lunch at Chiquitos in Sheffield. I am so pleased they are having some special treats too, as they thoroughly deserve them. The charities are fantastic at thinking about the siblings, when families are faced with a situation like ours.

Daddy has gone Christmas shopping and you and I are at home with Sian and Ioan, who came to visit. It was like old times, watching you two play. Ioan is walking and babbling away. Of course, it's sad that you are not yet at that stage, but you will get there.

Sunday 30 November 2014

Today you had a 'Daddy Day' while I went to Lincoln to meet my best friends Helen, Jen and Sonja for a Christmas present swap. It was good to see them but I missed you, very much. I've been with you every day since August and have never left you for a whole day. Before you became ill I did a few days back at work, as my maternity leave was coming to an end, and Daddy, Sian or Granny would look after you. But since August I have not left you for more than a couple of hours. So today seemed a very long day without you.

Of course, you were absolutely fine with Daddy, as I knew you would be. Granny and Uncle James came round and you all went for a walk. The community nurse came round at 3pm to do your G-CSF. Every mother finds it hard to leave their babies, if only for a short time, but the journey that we have been on these last few months has made me even more protective over you.

You were very excited when I got home. I put lots of presents under the tree, from Jen and Helen, Sonja, Nannie and Grandad. One a week to go until our Christmas Day – I hope Santa remembers to come early.

Monday 1 December 2014

Nannie is coming on the train from Skegness for the day. I think she is very excited about seeing you and playing with you.

Last time she visited, you became ill and we ended up sitting in the hospital waiting room all day. Not much of a fun visit for Nannie. It is going to be a busy day, because Grandad Geoff and Nanna Kaz, and maybe Steph and Selina are coming over later to drop off their Christmas presents.

I have been invited to a Body Shop party at the Smithy Pond pub this evening, organised by our friend Nicky. She has kindly offered to donate her commission to the charity night.

Tuesday 2 December 2014

We went back to hospital today for a glomerular filtration rate (GFR) test to check the function of your kidneys. You've had this before but you needed another one to check that the chemotherapy you have had so far hasn't affected your kidneys.

When we arrived on the ward, the play therapists were busy putting up all sorts of Christmas decorations. The characters from 'Frozen' visited the ward at 3.30pm, but we were on our way home by then – a shame. Our friends Benji and Louise met them, including the Olaf character, who was enormous. Think you might have been quite scared by him.

It was just a day visit today, but we are back to hospital again tomorrow for a longer stay and another MRI scan.

'GFR'

Glomerular filtration rate (GFR) is a test used to check how well the kidneys are working.

It estimates how much blood passes through the glomeruli each minute.

Glomeruli are the tiny filters in the kidneys that filter waste from the blood.

Wednesday 3 December 2014

These routine MRI scans always make me feel sick with apprehension. We won't get the results until tomorrow, so it will be another sleepless night for me. The best outcome would be that all signs of the tumour have disappeared, but this is probably unlikely. At the very least we can hope that it hasn't grown or changed since the last scan.

Thursday 4 December 2014

A busy and emotional day today and an overnight stay in hospital, with the MRI scan results. A Broviac line was fitted for the high dose chemotherapy session that starts Monday.

Seeing you in recovery with the new line fitted made me suddenly panic about what was to come next. I have been putting these fears to the back of my mind, preparing for our early Christmas, planning the charity night, and so on. But you are going to receive chemo at a much higher dose than before, which will inevitably make you very sick. Understanding the need is easy – to eliminate all remaining traces of the tumour so that it will not return – but having to bear the procedure with you is quite a different matter.

The high dose chemo will strip you of all your white blood cells. To help build them back again, you will also have a stem cell transplant, returning your own stem cells that were harvested from you weeks ago. This will to give your body the best possible chance of getting better. All these procedures will make you very poorly and susceptible to all sorts of infections and viruses, as your body won't be able to fight them.

You will need to be in isolation, so we will be in a separate room on the ward for at least four weeks. You won't be able to leave the room and we won't be able to have any visitors, including Jack and Molly. It is going to be horrible. I cannot 'make it go away', as a mother wants to be able to do… the guilt I feel is just enormous. I just hope it does what it needs to do and that you are able to cope with it. I don't think I have ever felt so nervous.

Friday 5 December 2014

The scan results were positive and the tumour has not grown. Thank goodness! It still looks the same as it did post-surgery in August. The consultant seemed quite pleased with the outcome.

We are going home later today, ready for our Christmas Eve tomorrow and Christmas Day on Sunday. Jack and Molly are getting very excited. I think you're wondering what all the fuss is about, and as for a tree with flashing lights on in the living room – you'll just think it's crazy!

Raffle prizes and auction lots for the charity night are coming in thick and fast. Two local artists, Mandy Payne and Katherine Rhodes, are both kindly donating pieces of artwork. Marie Smith, the owner of Waterbabies in Nottinghamshire, has also been in touch today. Two of her team, Lisa Bramley and Marie Copland, would like to donate some prizes. Neither actually taught you how to swim, but they have heard all about you from your own, wonderful, teacher Michelle Freeman. Lisa makes her own jewellery and Marie creates personalised homemade cushions. We now have a great variety of prizes and auction lots, and Daddy and I are overwhelmed by people's kindness and generosity.

Lucy's Special Christmas

✦

Father Christmas Comes Early

Saturday 6 December 2014

It's Christmas Eve. We were hoping for a whole day at home, but yesterday afternoon the doctor rang to say your blood count showed that you needed a blood transfusion. Daddy took you to Sheffield today. It was only about three hours but I had to be at the hairdresser's. I felt so guilty the whole time. I've never let you go to the hospital without me.

You were home again just after lunch, by which time I had managed to get all the Christmas dinner preparation done as well as keeping the appointment at the hairdresser's. I found myself getting tearful in the hairdresser's salon, so I picked up the local *Wings* magazine to distract my thoughts. Some weeks ago I'd been in touch with *Wings* and the *Derbyshire Times* to get some publicity for our charity event. I hadn't thought much more about it so as I flicked through the magazine it was a surprise to see your little face! It was the picture taken on our first walk out of hospital in September, with you in the pushchair and me giving you a little kiss on the cheek. Well done *Wings*!

Molly has a special job to do before bedtime tonight. Imogen, one of our friends in hospital, has made you some special reindeer food to sprinkle on our lawn. We are all hoping that Santa and Rudolph have remembered to make an early visit to Wingerworth...

Steve Miller, an ex-colleague of Daddy's, has also been in touch today to let us know that his music and entertainment night last night raised £1036. Daddy managed to go to the show with Uncle James and they said it was a great success. Uncle James won a bottle of wine in the raffle and has given it to me, so everyone benefits.

What a wonderful thing Steve has done, raising so much money for the Children's Hospital Charity.

Sunday 7 December 2014

Today is our special Christmas Day. I received so many 'Merry Christmas' wishes on my Facebook page this morning it really did feel like Christmas Day. Our living room was completely full of presents and it took ages to open them all. We were all truly spoilt with some lovely gifts: Jack and Molly had lots of games, dolls, sweets, books and clothes. You had a toy garage and cars from Mummy and Daddy, and Santa brought you a push trolley with bricks, clothes, baby toys, puzzles and much more.

Mummy was given some Pandora charms for the bracelet that Sian gave her: there was a special 'L' charm for Lucy (of course) and a very special 'Hope' one from Daddy. Helen, Jen and Sonja bought me the 'Best Friends' one. So I now have four special charms on my lovely bracelet. Daddy got a new PlayStation game, which will be useful when he is in the hospital room while you are sleeping.

Granny Sheena and Uncle James came for lunch and stayed for the afternoon. I cooked a big Christmas Dinner with all the trimmings and we were all suitably stuffed by the afternoon. You were tucked up, fast asleep, by 6.30pm, tired out with all of the excitement of the day.

As lovely as today was, I hope that our next Christmas Day will be so very different for us all. We will make it the best Christmas ever, I promise.

Tomorrow is the first day of the biggest challenge you'll ever have to face...

High Dose Chemotherapy

✦

The Biggest Challenge So Far

Monday 8 December 2014

We said a very sad goodbye to Jack and Molly this morning. It will be a few weeks before you are able to see them again. It is so hard to explain to them what is happening to you. Molly finds it difficult. I think that Jack, being a bit older, understands better why you have to go away again. I hope they will still manage to enjoy the real Christmas when it comes.

I spent the morning packing our bags, ironing and putting away all those Christmas presents. We set off for hospital at about 2pm, with more tears as we said goodbye to Marjorie and David next door. I can't tell you how sick I feel or how scared I am. Who knows what the next few weeks are going to bring?

We arrived at hospital thinking we would be on the main ward for a couple of days but we were given a separate room straight away. I was relieved, as I knew that I would be crying again if I had to talk to any of the other mothers. I just couldn't face them today, even though they are the best ones to understand what I am going through, and they are all absolutely lovely.

We are back in Room 7, which is where we were when we first got moved here from S2 Ward in September. I remember feeling sick and worried then. Maybe Room 7 is destined to be our lucky room? Let's hope so.

I have been busy decorating your room, trying not to think about things too much. The one helpful thing about all of this is that you are so little. You don't fully understand what is going on and that is a blessing. I don't know where I would begin if I had to explain these last few months to you.

Auntie Claire has given you a miniature Christmas tree with a special fairy decoration and a Rudolph soft toy. My cousin Debs gave you a 'Santa stop here for Lucy' sign that I have hung up above your cot.

Sian and Ioan gave you a gorgeous pink blanket for Christmas. It has your name, birth weight and date on it, and it is going to keep you warm in here. Ioan has the same type of blanket, in blue. It is a very special present and will be a lasting treasure. We will take it on our first buggy walk with Ioan when we are back at home. That is what I shall think every time I wrap you in the blanket.

Your room looks cosy and as cheerful as I can make it. There are lots of Christmas toys to keep you busy for the next four weeks. You seem happy and blissfully unaware of what is really happening. So Day 1, of however many, is nearly over...

Tomorrow you will start the high dose chemotherapy. We just have to hope it does what it needs to do.

Wednesday 10 December 2014

The chemo infusion went without incident. You were a bit sleepless last night but you slept for nearly three hours this morning, and then another hour late afternoon. It seems a bit too soon for the drugs to be making you sleepy; maybe it is because of the high dose? You've also been sick today.

Haseeb's mum popped in today and brought you a present of a little Peppa Pig toy. Haseeb is a lovely boy and has been in hospital an awful long time. Benji and Louise have also come in today. Benji has leukaemia and has been in and out of hospital since the summer. I have become good friends with his mum and his family. Benji's nanny came over one day when you were about to go to theatre. She held my hand and gave me a hug. We had not long met and I was embarrassed that I had got upset in front of her, but she was just so thoughtful. I was on my own that day, as Daddy was at work, and I will never forget how kind she was to me. We have made some good friends in hospital. Louise and the whole of the Robinsons are a lovely family. They have said they would like to come to our Charity Auction Night. Benji's Auntie Lindsey has also donated £100 of John Lewis vouchers as raffle prize – wonderful!

In the evenings we are trying to keep you awake longer than usual as you need to have four baths a day. All our well-established routines have been abandoned. One of the side effects of the drug called Thiatepin that you having at high dose is that it can damage your skin, so we have to wash it frequently. Thiatepin can almost burn the skin. You hate the baths and cry all the way through. It is hard to do with all your line and drips. I hate it; it is like someone ripping my heart out. It takes two of us and a nurse to bathe you whilst holding up all your wires etc. You used to love baths and swimming and I just hope this experience doesn't change that.

Thursday 11 December 2014

You will be having a lumbar puncture today, but it will be your last one ever. Hurray! You have been having them every two weeks, so it's good that it will soon stop. Daddy is going to get Jack and Molly and have them at the house for the night, which is really important for them. So it will just be you and me for most of the day and the evening. We will see Daddy tomorrow. No doubt you will be very sleepy after your trip to theatre.

Friday 12 December 2014

Daddy picked the wrong evening to be at home last night. Benji's Nanna, Leigh, brought a delicious home-cooked meal into hospital for my tea. What a welcome surprise! They are such a brave family, going through their own difficult times, yet they still think of others. Leigh also bought us a musical Christmas tree tin of biscuits. I'll save the biscuits for Daddy, but I know that you'll have fun with the musical tin.

Players from Sheffield Wednesday Football Club have visited the ward today to cheer up the children who will be in hospital over Christmas. They were handing out goodie bags and although you are not particularly interested in one (nor would Jack be, as Sheffield United fan), the play therapist kindly brought one over to us. I've decided to use it as an auction lot for the Charity night, along with some tickets to a game that we have been given by the Children's Hospital Charity. Gemma from the charity has been especially helpful, giving us tickets to a Sheffield United game and organising various leaflets, a banner and some charity T-shirts for helpers to wear on the night.

You are not at all well today. I can't bear to see you like this. You were very unsettled last night too and today you just want to sleep on my shoulder or have cuddles. It is absolutely heart breaking seeing you this poorly and being helpless to make it go away.

However, on a positive note, I have just realised that today is possibly your last day of chemotherapy. We have already been told that you will not be able to have any more chemotherapy because it would damage your body. A little bit of me is nervous. As much I don't want you to suffer anymore from the side-effects of chemo, I hope you have had enough to stop the tumour from coming back.

But let's focus on the positives of today… no more chemo. Brilliant!

The best view comes after the hardest climb.

Saturday 13 December 2014

It was another unsettled night, with cuddles nearly every hour. I don't mind that at all, but am a bit tired today. You are still very lethargic and being sick. Even your medicines came back up earlier and you are only having tiny amounts of milk on the continuous feed. I am so sorry you are having to go through this. I think it will be another day of cuddles today.

I've have just read a Facebook message by Sarah Osbourne, the owner of Chuckle Chimps, the soft play hire company that we hoped to have at your 1st Birthday party. Her message says that instead of sending all her customers a Christmas card this year, she would like to donate the money to the group of charities that we are supporting at the Charity Night. She wrote a little bit about you and how your party had to be cancelled. This is such a kind thing to do. So many people are still thinking of you, Lucy… xxx

I'm going to Meadowhall today to meet a coach from Skegness. Hannah, who lives next door to Nannie, works at Barclays Bank in Skegness, and she has asked colleagues to collect items for Treetops: things like kitchen and toilet rolls, washing up liquid etc. How generous of her to find time to organise a collection. I will sort one box for the PACT house as they need similar things, and that is where Daddy is staying now.

I might have a quick visit to the Pandora shop whilst I'm at Meadowhall. Granny gave me some money for Christmas and I would like to buy two more charms: a good luck one and a baby girl one (I can't think why I might want those!).

Come on Lucy – keep fighting… xxx

Sunday 14 December 2014

You snuggled me most of last night. Every time I put you in the cot you wanted to be picked up again. I think we now know why: this morning the doctor explained that your gums were extremely sore (another side-effect of the chemo) and he suggested that you have regular Ora-morph. I found this upsetting, since the last time you were on this drug was after the surgery in August. It dawned on me how much pain you must be suffering.

You are extremely tired today. You had an x-ray to check your feeding tube was in the right place as it wasn't testing correctly, which implies it may be sitting in the wrong position, and that can potentially be very dangerous. Daddy is spending the day with Jack and Molly. You and I will be spending most of the day napping and cuddling. At least the four baths a day have finished now.

It is another big day tomorrow – stem cell transplant.

Monday 15 December 2014

Your cousin, Emily, has her 6th Birthday today. I have been putting regular posts and photos of you on Facebook for our friends and family, but I won't do so today. You are not looking at all well and your skin is bright red from the Thiatepin. You have pretty much lost all of you hair now too and you have even lost your eyebrows and eye lashes.

We had a better night last night but you are still very weak and tired. You are awake for short periods only and you want lots of cuddles. The doctors have increased your morphine dose today, which has made you even sleepier. I have been feeling very tearful today, seeing you so poorly. My little girl seems to be deteriorating in front of me. I desperately want you to get better, to get through this horrible, horrible time, and that you will never remember any of it.

The stem cell transplant started today, which will help your body to make its own white blood cells again. You don't have any neutrophils at the moment, which is why you are so ill. They have been completely destroyed by chemo. You will have another transplant session tomorrow, and then we have to wait. You will inevitably need platelet transfusions, blood transfusions, antibiotics, the full works; and if your temperature rises too high, there will be more fluids and morphine.

Your mouth is extremely red and sore, which must be causing you so much pain. It is absolutely heart breaking. The morphine should be helping a bit, making you sleepy but without pain. You have developed something called Mucositis. It is a painful inflammation and ulceration of the mucous membranes lining the mouth, throat and into the gut. It is another adverse side-effect of the chemotherapy.

Daddy is here and I was able to take a ten minute break to deliver the boxes to Treetops and the PACT house. The staff there seemed really pleased with the donations.

Our friends Louise and Benji have gone home today for Christmas. They are due back again on 30th December and will be in hospital for the New Year, like us. I am pleased Benji will be at home, although we shall miss them. It is nice to have five minutes out of the hospital room to talk to someone.

Daddy has been keeping himself busy, decorating the walls in your room. The play therapists gave us some special pens that can be used to write or draw on the walls. Patients and their families often write messages or draw pictures. It is a great idea. Daddy had the wonderful idea of creating a Christmas scene for you, and he has done an amazing job. He really is quite talented. He has drawn a snowman, a penguin, a little wooden cabin, a moose, and even Santa on his skis coming down the side of the mountain. I don't think you have particularly noticed it, but when you are older I will show the photograph, and you will be able to see how Daddy tried to make your room feel a bit Christmassy. The nurses keep praising his drawings and I think he's secretly quite pleased with himself. It does look good.

Tuesday 16 December 2014

It has been another rotten day and night. When you lie down, the secretions gather in your mouth and they have to be sucked out with a suction machine. I can't bear watching, as it obviously painful and you hate it. Sometimes I have to hold you so that the nurses can do it properly. It is painful, distressing and I am so sorry, poppet, for all this suffering.

You had the second lot of stem cells transplanted today. That has all gone to plan, but you are still neutropenic and will probably need a platelet transfusion in the next day. Platelets help the blood clot. So, because you mouth sometimes bleeds and is very sore from the mucositis is it especially important that you have enough in your body. The morphine has been increased again to try to make you more comfortable. You are having all your drugs intravenously because you are being sick a lot.

All in all it has been another horrible day for you. I just want this to end. You really are at rock bottom. Please don't give up little Lucy… xxxxx

The hardest part of being a parent is watching a child go through something really tough and not be able to fix it for them.
All I am doing is all I can do.

Wednesday 17 December 2014

You are going to start something called Total Parenteral Nutrition (TPN) later today. You are not getting enough nutrition from the small quantities of milk that you are managing to swallow. You were supposed to start TPN yesterday but your electrolytes were too unstable. When is this ever going to end?

Thursday 18 December 2014

Little did I know as I wrote the diary entry yesterday morning that it would be the most terrifying day of my life…

Daddy was with Jack and Molly at home. You were very sleepy all morning, making it even more difficult for you to struggle with the secretions in your mouth. You needed a lot of suction.

At one point I was in the room alone with you when you started spluttering and then suddenly you went very floppy and blue in the face. It happened very quickly but I knew you were struggling to breathe. I pulled the emergency cord and all the doctors and nurses came rushing in. They just appeared from nowhere.

'Total Parenteral Nutrition'

Parenteral nutrition provides liquid nutrients, including carbohydrates, proteins, fats, vitamins, minerals and electrolytes, through a needle inserted into a vein.

TPN is used for patients who cannot or should not get their nutrition through eating.

It was very frightening but Dr Hannah and Dr Dan were calm and professional, as were all the nurses. One of them held me as I stood shaking and crying uncontrollably in the corner. I thought I was going to lose you. They helped with your breathing and gradually you started to come round. Then I heard you whimper and felt enormous relief. I rang Daddy to ask him to come back straight away.

The doctors decided to do an immediate CT scan to check that all was well, but as we began to take you from your bed it happened again. I was holding you and Dr Hannah was carrying some equipment; as she held the door open for us I heard you splutter again and felt you go floppy. I screamed and they flung you onto the bed in the treatment room, which is right by the double doors. They immediately put an oxygen mask over your face and gave you suction.

Dr Hannah pulled the emergency cord and all the doctors and nurses came dashing in again with the resuscitation trolley. I couldn't believe it was happening. There was a mucus plug in your throat that had blocked your airways. The Ward Sister, Hilary, looked after me this time, trying to get me to sit down. She said I had gone that pale and she thought I might faint, but I just wanted to be near you. It was absolutely terrifying. Once you had recovered you were taken back to our room. Dr Hannah didn't leave us, even though I knew she was due to go home.

If twice wasn't enough, you had another episode later in the afternoon. Daddy was back with us, but it was after 5.30pm and some of the doctors had left. Nonetheless, when we pulled the emergency cord, doctors and nurses flew in from everywhere. They get alerted wherever they are in the hospital and they speed to the room. One doctor dashed in, wearing his jeans – I remembered him as one of the operating theatre anaesthetists. He was clearly on his way home when the alarm sounded. He was brilliant with you.

It was decided very quickly that you needed to go to the Intensive Care Unit (ICU). You needed one-to-one nursing, which is not always possible on M3 Ward. Also, having had three emergencies in one afternoon, you need to have breathing apparatus immediately at hand. I remember feeling so scared as we went to the ICU. What would happen there?

We hadn't been in intensive care before. Even after the main operations you were placed on the HDU, not the ICU. There was quite a young nurse looking after you and I remember thinking, crikey – I just hope she is experienced enough to help you. What if it you stopped breathing again?

I felt guilty for doubting the skills and expertise of this young nurse, who was there all night with you. She was absolutely brilliant and I will never forget her. She watched you all the time, gave you regular suction to prevent any more mucus blockages and made sure you remained stable. When you finally fell asleep, I sat in the chair and tried to sleep myself. I was exhausted but I knew I couldn't fall asleep. I dare not sleep. I just had to keep watching you, to make sure you were safe.

That was last night and today we are still in the ICU; but I think we'll be back on M3 before the day is over. Your breathing seems to be under control and the regular suction is helping to prevent any more blockages. The main problem today is a high temperature. You are sleeping most of the time and I hope that means you are comfortable and not in any pain.

It is midday now and we are just waiting for the ICU doctors to do their rounds and to hear from M3 that they have enough nurses for us, as ideally you need one with you all the time.

H.O.P.E …Hold On, Pain Ends

The Long Stay in Hospital

✦

Very Weak... No End in Sight?

Friday 19 December 2014

We were moved back to M3 at about 8pm last night. One of the nurses, Claire, gave me a big hug to welcome us back. You were very unsettled during the night and still needed lots of suction, but we got through it.

We had a visit from Santa today, who delivered a present from the Friends of PACT. They have raised money to buy Christmas presents for all the children on M3 Ward. Your present was a push-along toy trolley with a doll inside it. A really big present. Thank you to PACT, again.

Becky, one of the play workers brought you another surprise. Asda donate various toys and things to the hospital over Christmas, and Becky has to sort through them all and decide how best to hand them out. Very cleverly, she chose a giant sized Teddy for you. He is enormous and sits in the chair. I am sure you will love him.

Then when Daddy went back to the PACT house a bit later on he found a hamper for us in his room, again donated by the Friends of PACT. It is splendid. There are all sorts of things in there – cakes, biscuits, chocolates. It will keep me and Daddy supplied over Christmas. There really are some wonderfully kind people in the world, and we are so grateful for what they have done for us.

So, although you are still very poorly, it was nice to have a couple of things to cheer us up today.

Saturday 20 December 2014

You seem more poorly today than yesterday. I don't know why. You have needed a lot of help with your breathing, including suction and even the oxygen mask at times. It is absolutely horrendous watching you go through this. I never imagined it would be this bad. I certainly did not know what to expect when Vicki, the consultant, first told us about this stage of the treatment. I was not prepared for how bad it was going to be. We have even had the ICU doctors come to see whether you should be back there, if M3 Ward cannot provide one nurse to be with you all the time.

Sunday 21 December 2014

Last night was tricky again, although we had a nurse with us all the time. She was brilliant. You are being treated with a nebuliser every four hours, to help loosen your secretions and make it easier for you to breathe. The nebuliser delivers asthma medication by turning it into a mist to be inhaled through a face mask or mouthpiece. It seems to help a little, so we hope you'll need less suction. You are getting lots of high temperatures too, so you need regular paracetamol.

I wish I knew when the end was in sight. Sleeping or cuddling is how you spend most of your days and you are not in the mood for smiling or playing. I miss that little smile of yours. Things can't get any worse for you right now. I never imagined this is how we would be spending your second Christmas. Next year is going to be so different – I promise.

Monday 22 December 2014

It is two weeks today since we came for our long stay in hospital. What a time we've had. You are still very sleepy but you have managed to sit up in your cot for a little while today and play for a bit. It was encouraging to see.

Tuesday 23 December 2014

A very sleepless night last night for us both, with cuddles for most of the night. I am shattered.

There was a big delivery of presents yesterday. My friend Claire (Oliver's mummy) offered to bring some boxes of toys that had been donated to Autoworld Chesterfield for their Toy Appeal.

Becky Measures, the Peak FM radio presenter who is supporting our charity auction, wanted Lucy to have some of the toys. We have picked out some wooden bricks for you, a toy car for Benji and a doll's set for Imogen. I have given the other toys to the play workers to sort for Christmas presents. The hospital has received so many toys it really is quite overwhelming, but so very generous of the public.

You have reached a new low point today and it is horrendous. As one of the nurses removed one of your dressings, it ripped off a layer of your skin leaving it red raw. It was unavoidable, the dressing needed removing and I don't think the nurses realised just how weak your skin had become. It was deeply upsetting for all of us. I couldn't even give you a big cuddle because you were in so much pain. Absolutely heart breaking to watch. The nurses have been in touch with the Burns Unit, who will let you have some of their special dressings so that this doesn't happen again.

Your little lips are sore and bleeding today too. This is just awful. What else can go wrong? How much more pain can you endure? How much more can the three of us can cope with? I am so, so sorry this is happening to you, my precious little girl.

Christmas Eve

I hope you never have another Christmas Eve like this one. You have been extremely poorly today, struggling with your breathing. The HDU/ICU have been informed in case we need to be transferred. You need the oxygen mask close by you all the time and you have developed a dry, sore throat. They think your airways have been narrowed.

One of the doctors who came to assess you in the night said it might be something called 'Stridor'. This is all down to the high dose chemo which has stripped the lining of your mouth, throat and gut. It must be agony for you. The morphine has been increased yet again.

Daddy is allowed to stay in our room tonight, so at least we can share cuddle duty tonight.

Christmas Day

Well we've already had our family Christmas Day this year. That's what I need to keep telling myself. Just as well, as you slept for most of this one, bless you. You were awake at 4am and wanted to play for a little bit, which was lovely. Daddy and I took turns to cuddle you all night. The nurses were creeping round at 5am. I think they were helping Santa to deliver presents to the few children who were in hospital last night. Spending Christmas in hospital is sad for any child, but the nurses go to so much trouble to try and make it a special day.

'Stridor'

An abnormal, high pitched, musical breathing sound, caused by a blockage in the throat or larynx. It is most often heard when taking in a breath.

In young children, stridor is a sign of airway blockage. It must be treated immediately to prevent the airway becoming closed.

Santa came onto the ward in the morning and brought you a lovely wooden train. You had a couple of presents delivered in the night – a wooden xylophone and another wooden animal toy set. They are gorgeous toys and we shall treasure them.

Daddy and I were even able to have a Christmas Dinner, served on the ward. At about 3pm Daddy went to collect Jack and Molly to take them to Uncle James' house where they are going to have tea with Granny. Then Daddy will be back later tonight.

I was hoping to show you some of your new toys but you are blissfully sleeping. It's the most settled you've been in a few days and you have actually gone down in your cot to sleep, which is a first in a long time. I won't disturb you just yet.

All in all it's been a very emotional day and the strangest Christmas I have ever had, that's for sure. Having cuddles with you this morning was lovely but having to hold the oxygen mask over your face at the same time was particularly upsetting. My precious little baby girl, who is just 15 months old tomorrow, should not be having to deal with this, especially not on their second Christmas.

2014 has turned out to be the most challenging year of our lives for me and Daddy. Here is to a happy and healthier 2015…

Boxing Day 2014

Happy 15-month-birthday my gorgeous girl! You still need the oxygen mask and your skin is still extremely sore. It doesn't really feel like Boxing Day; I just want this year to be over. I have so much hope for 2015.

Saturday 27 December 2014

We have had some good news today about your blood count. You have started to make a few more neutrophils. If this continues, your body will be able to repair and recover much more quickly. The skin on your face is looking better today. It is just the back of the neck that is still bright red and making you itch.

Daddy has been back to the house today to see Jack and Molly and to pick up some post. I have a special surprise from my friend Louise, who lives in Norwich. We used to teach in the same school a few years ago and have remained friends ever since. She has bought me tickets to see Take That with her in June. How exciting! I used to be a big fan when I was about 14 years old and I still love them now. I wonder when you read this whether you will have heard of them?

I forgot to write up the diary on Boxing Day. I was feeling too sad to do much writing. But it snowed really hard and the night shift nurses struggled to get into Sheffield. Two of the nurses, Sian and Carly, who had been here all day, offered to stay and work through the night shift. They must have been absolutely shattered. They said they would take it in turns to have a sleep during the night but they never did, so they both worked a 24hr shift. That really goes above and beyond and we are so grateful to them. Sian is one of the more senior nurses and usually just works the day shifts. She did your stem cell transplant. Apparently she hasn't done a night shift in years – I don't suppose she'll forget this one in a hurry.

Sian was brilliant with you and made you really comfortable with your breathing etc. You had the best night sleep you've had in a long time. So I was secretly pleased she stayed to look after you but I was concerned how exhausted she would be feeling. She is also a priest and was supposed to be writing her sermon on the Saturday. I hope she slept instead.

The snow is still on the ground at the moment, it is icy cold, although there has not been any fresh snow. It has made me think I can't wait to build your first snowman with you. Another memory that we need to make.

Sunday 28 December 2014

More good news this morning. Your face is looking heaps better now and your neutrophil levels have increased again. Maybe things are finally on the up. You require daily platelet infusions and this will keep us in hospital for a while yet. Thank goodness for all those people who donate platelets. Apparently it's a bit different to a blood donor but many people still do it. When I see one of the motorbikes that transport the blood to the hospital it make me feel very emotional.

They have continued to decrease your morphine dose, so you'll soon start to feel more alert. You've been sitting up and playing a little bit more than usual this morning although you are having an extra-long nap now. Daddy is reading his mountain bike magazine and I might start reading one of my books. It's something I have not done for weeks, so maybe I'm beginning to relax.

Keep making those neutrophils, poppet, as it making you feel so much better day by day. Love you loads, xxx

Monday 29 December 2014

And another positive start to the day – you are now officially out of isolation. It means we can have visitors again. I bet you can't wait to see Jack and Molly and Granny.

You have made more neutrophils and are no longer neutropenic or at high risk of infection. We still need to be careful, but this is definitely a step in the right direction. Even the smiles and giggles are coming back. Daddy got them first but I don't really mind. I am just so happy you are starting to feel better.

Today we have been in hospital for exactly three weeks. It is going a lot quicker than I thought it would. It's definitely helped having Daddy here. I'm not sure how I could have coped being here on my own all day.

Tuesday 30 December 2014

You were a bit restless last night. I think you have a lot of dried blood in your tummy. You are coughing most of it up but it is making you sick and you're retching a little.

They have inserted your feeding tube again today so that you can start to have milk again. You need to be back on full milk feeds before you can go home, so the sooner we start this the better. I have a feeling it could take a while, though.

Imogen's mum, Clair, called to see us today and brought us some chocolates and a bottle of wine. Although you are feeling a lot better than you were, I suppose you do look quite poorly, and Clair was quite upset when she first saw you. To me you seem so much better.

Hopefully, we'll see our friends Louise and Benji later, as they are coming in again today for treatment.

Wednesday 31 December 2014 – New Year's Eve

You are getting better every day and you have started to have small amounts of milk again. Your skin is almost back to normal too now.

I think I'll have the wine Clair brought me yesterday. Daddy has a beer, so we'll order a takeaway and call it our New Year's Eve treat. Not the wildest New Year's Eve I've ever had but I don't really care. Seeing you improve each day is the best New Year's present we could ask for.

Thursday 1 January 2015 – New Year's Day

The milk is making you sick and you are coughing up little bits of blood. This is probably due to the damage to your stomach lining. We've had to reduce the milk feed, although you are only having 5mls an hour.

I hope this doesn't keep us in hospital too long. You need a bit longer for your skin to heal, and then you will be ready to come home. We can't wait for that…

Friday 2 January 2015

The play therapists are taking down the Christmas decorations and it looks so bare on the ward. We have been making the tree that was a present from Tamara. The idea is to collect fingerprints from all the doctors and nurses. The roots give you strength (Mummy, Daddy, Jack and Molly and other family members), the branches support you and the fingerprints are for all the people that help and guide you through life. So we've been asking all the doctors, nurses and friends we have made in hospital to make a print.

More smiles and playing in the cot again today. I am beginning to feel so much more positive.

Saturday 3 January 2015

You slept better last night, but we were woken at 4.30am by the doctor who needed to check your fluid levels. So, by 5am we were both wide awake.

We were allowed to take you out in your pushchair for half an hour this morning. We haven't done this since you came into hospital on the 8th December. It was lovely to be out with you, even though the weather was pretty miserable. You were fine under the rain cover but Daddy and I got soaking wet.

You are still struggling with tiny amounts of milk and we've no idea when that might improve. Your tummy must still be very sore – the side effect of the chemo.

We have added a few more fingerprints to the tree today. We still need to ask your consultants, Dr Vicki Lee and Dr Dan. I'm sure they'll join in the fun.

Monday 5 January 2015

It is four weeks today since we arrived at hospital. The doctors originally said we might be in for about four weeks, but I think we will be here for at least another week. We've still a long way to go with feeding.

We received some good news today that has cheered me up enormously. The charity, Amy's Retreat, have offered us a family holiday at Center Parcs in Sherwood Forest. I believe that our names were put forward by CLIC Sargent. We will go for a long weekend on Friday 27th February. I'm already excited at the thought of having some family time together. We will definitely have to run another charity night, as there are several other charities that have supported us, but aren't on the beneficiary list for this year's charity auction.

Tuesday 6 January 2015

Daddy is getting a few phone calls about possible job offers. We all hope that he'll get an interview soon.

Your milk feeds have been increased slightly. Vicki, the consultant, said they would try to reduce the number of intravenous medicines you are receiving, in preparation for going home.

You are much happier today. Daddy made you giggle, which gave you hiccups. Thanks Daddy!

Thursday 8 January 2015

Good News Day! This morning Vicki spoke about planning to come home, probably early next week. I can't quite believe it. We need to increase your milk feeds to 30mls an hour, from today's level of 20mls per hour. You also need to go another day without a platelet infusion, otherwise we will have to return to hospital to have them. So get working Lucy!

The second bit of good news is that Daddy has been invited to a couple of job interviews. If he can be in work again by February then we'll be OK.

Only 22 days to go now until the auction night and still so much to do. If I'm feeling brave I might go back to the house tomorrow to sort out a few things. The conservatory is full of donations for the raffle and auction. When I started planning the charity night I didn't imagine it would involve so much work but it has given me a real buzz, organising and watching it develop. I think we will raise some serious money. Friends and family have been incredibly generous and we could not have done it without them.

You are looking really well again today. You had a long sleep last night and you've been playing and giggling all day. What more could we ask for?

We're allowed to take you out again for half an hour. We just need it to stop raining and for you to wake up from your nap.

Friday 9 January 2015

You had a Daddy Day today while I went home – the first time for over a month. It felt quite strange and I really didn't like being there without you.

Daddy has had a good day with you. He kept sending me videos of you playing and giggling. You are doing really well. Still sick a couple of times a day, but otherwise you are much improved.

Saturday 10 January 2015

Uncle Mark, Auntie Alison and Katie were due to visit today but they all have colds so they must stay away. Daddy went to see 'The Hobbit' at the cinema last night with Uncle James. It is good for him to do 'normal' things. The weather isn't very nice for your half-hour outing but we'll get the rain cover on and go anyway. Daddy and I go a bit stir crazy in here otherwise.

Sunday 11 January 2015

Jack, Molly, Granny and Uncle James came to visit today. You were very excited to see them. We went for a walk in the park but it was bitterly cold so we weren't out for long.

We have been busy finishing your tree, and have fingerprints of all the doctors and nurses.

You are still sick a couple of times a day but otherwise you are much better. I think we might be able to go home tomorrow...

Home Again

✦

Slight Improvement, Still No Swallow

Monday 12 January 2015

We're allowed to go home. Hooray! It's taken Daddy about five trips to and from the car to empty the room. We had so much stuff in here.

We said goodbye to the nurses and I felt very emotional. We have had the most exhausting, emotionally draining five weeks of our lives, devastated by what you have had to suffer. We hope that the treatment has been worth it and has worked its magic. If all this was in vain, I would never forgive myself for putting you through it. But I must stop talking like this – we have a new start to our bright future together. You've overcome so much and if it is not quite over, I know that we'll get you through it, together as a family, making you stronger each day.

You are loved by very many people and one day you'll be able to get glimpse of that in these diaries, or by looking back at all of the cards, presents, photos and videos that we have collected for you along the way. I know your fight isn't over and there will be many more obstacles in our path, but going home today makes me believe that we have managed to get over the biggest hurdle. The last five weeks have been an enormous challenge for you. Your body has suffered but you have shown such strength and bravery. You are already climbing back up that mountain. Your family is immensely proud of you.

We finally got home at about 8pm. You fell fast asleep on the way home and we managed to get you straight into your cot... until midnight, when you were wide awake again, xxx

Tuesday 13 January 2015

It's Auntie Claire's birthday today. She said that her best present was to hear that you were coming home.

Daddy has a job interview this afternoon in Nottingham. He has another on Thursday and one more next Tuesday. Hopefully he'll have the pick of more than one of these.

You are happy, playing with all your new Christmas toys. You love the letterbox from Granny and the garage that Daddy and I gave you. It a lovely sight and I am so very happy to be home where we belong.

Wednesday 14 January 2015

Rachel, one of our community nurses had to come out to re-insert your feeding tube. She did a full blood count too, so we'll find out later if we need to go back into hospital for more platelets. I'm half-expecting that we will. Rachel and the other community nurses, Tracey, Louise, Michelle, Rosie Alison and Paul, have been absolutely wonderful. I have lost count of the number of times we have had to call them in the early hours of the morning or late at night to come to re-insert your feeding tube. I hate watching the procedure and I know I am no help at all. I will never get used to seeing you so distressed. It is horrid. The nurses are always patient with us. They find the time to stop and chat too, if I'm having a tearful day. I can never thank them enough for what they do.

Rachel is our Sheffield-based key worker, who supported us a lot when we were in hospital. She is like a mother hen to us all. Today she offered the kindest, nicest thing… I have mentioned the auction to her, and a couple of times I have said how worried I was about leaving Lucy for the night. The plan is for her to stay with Granny, but knowing how frequently the feeding tubes comes out or how often she can still be sick, I have been worried that it would be a heavy responsibility for Granny. Well, Rachel has offered to look after you on the charity night so that I can relax, knowing that you'll have a nurse there should anything happen.

When she told me, I burst into tears and hugged her. It also means that Granny can now come to the charity night too. I have been worrying about this for weeks. It is a great relief. I shall have to buy Rachel a special Thank You present.

Daddy has a second interview tomorrow. Good news all round.

Thursday 15 January 2015

As expected, we are off to hospital for a platelets transfusion. I don't think I knew what platelets were before you started treatment. Now we talk about them all the time.

'PEG'

Percutaneous endoscopic gastrostomy (PEG) is an endoscopic medical procedure in which a tube is passed into a patient's stomach through the abdominal wall.

It is most commonly to provide a means of feeding when oral intake is not adequate.

We also saw Vicki, who was delighted at your progress. You are going to have a PEG fitted in February, as this is a better long-term solution for your feeding.

I am not sure how much more you can take of feeding tubes being re-inserted nearly every day. The tube comes out every time you are sick, which has been very frequently.

No more tubes on your face will be lovely. I know the PEG may come with its own set of problems but it must be better than the NG tubes. The PEG will also be hidden discretely under your clothes, so it's another step towards you 'looking well'.

It's something that I hate about the NG tube when we are out and about. People don't half stare.

Sunday 18 January 2015

You had a lovely day at home yesterday, playing with me and Daddy. Jack and Molly are with us today and they love playing with you too.

Uncle Mark, Auntie Alison and Katie visited today and you had great fun with Uncle Mark, who always makes you giggle.

Rachel the nurse came to take another blood count. Will we need to go into hospital again tomorrow for platelets I wonder?

2015 - A Year Filled With Hope

In February 2015, as a special treat for being so brave, our dear friend Tamara sent these lovely balloons for you in the post. Balloons are a firm favourite with you now and I wonder if this is where it all started?

A lunch date with Jake at February half term. I think your lack of hair was a surprise but he was as kind and as sensitive as ever.

Lucy's 'Tree of Love', an idea from Tamara. We collected fingerprints of the nurses and doctors on M3 as well as friends and family. Each fingerprint has the 'owner's' name alongside it.

Lucy's Tree of Love

December 2014

We found a warm welcome at our lodge at Center Parcs, Sherwood Forest, and were quick to take a refreshing walk around the park.

Mother's Day lunch out in the Peak District with Mummy, Daddy and Granny Sheena.

Lucy's tea room in the Cotswolds! We just had to refresh with tea and cake here.

Our dear friend Tamara participated in the 'Muddy Challenge' in Crowle, North Lincolnshire where she lives. It was a 10k obstacle course through lakes, mud and even a skip! She trained hard and completed the run in a very fast time, raising over £500 for Ellie's Fund, The Brain Tumour Trust.

Here you are with your friend Imogen who we met in hospital in September 2014. She was diagnosed with Leukaemia, at about the same time that you began your chemotherapy. You were both in theatre on this day and saw each other when you returned to the Recovery ward.

A Father's Day lunch with Jack, Molly, Daddy and Mummy at the Peacock , Owler Bar, near Sheffield.

Your friend Benji – the poster boy for Make It Better campaign with Sheffield Children's Hospital Charity.

With Uncle James and Taylah.

Above: During our week's holiday in Dorset we visited Emily and Thomas, Auntie Claire and Uncle Ben at their campsite, just outside Bridport at West Bay.

Below: With cousins Taylah, Jaiden and Calli on a rainy bank holiday in Mablethorpe.

Monday 19 January 2015

Your blood count was not as low as we feared so you have an extra day at home. We saw Sian, Ioan, Katie, Thomas, Sarah, Oliver and Millie. Ioan and Thomas are both walking around confidently. Although it is wonderful to see them developing as they should, I can't pretend it is not hard watching you, who are just a few weeks younger, not doing those things.

Tuesday 20 January 2015

Off to the hospital for another platelet transfusion, although the levels were not as low as everyone was expecting. That's fantastic news and means that your body is starting to make more and more of them.

Another interview for Daddy today...

Thursday 22 January 2015

I heard some terrible news while we were in hospital yesterday. A young boy called Todd, about 10 or 11 years old, who had been suffering with cancer for a long time, has sadly passed away. The news really upset me, realising just how frightening this nasty disease can be. Todd was incredibly strong, as was his mum. He actually looked very well when we were in hospital a couple of months ago. I am stunned and can't stop thinking about him.

Friday 23 January 2015

I am meeting Bernie and Becky again today. James Lewis, the auctioneer, has unfortunately pulled out of the charity night.

We are enjoying having you at home. The physiotherapist is visiting today. Daddy has a second interview for a job. I think that it is the one that he would really like.

I am busy every evening and during your naptimes trying to finish off all the auction plans. We have just 20 tickets left for the charity night, which means that we have sold 180. That's not bad for my first fundraising event. In addition, we have sold almost 5000 raffle tickets, which means we've raised £5000 already. One week to go to the big event...

Your cold is back with a vengeance; a very green snotty nose. You're very sleepy today too. Lots of Calpol and cuddles to help you feel better. You have gone back onto three-hourly bolus feeds now as opposed to the continuous feed.

This is excellent progress and another step in the right direction. I was not comfortable with the continuous feed at night time, now that you are becoming more active in your cot. I was always scared you would get the tubes wrapped around you.

Monday 26 January to Thursday 29 January 2015

Lots of auction preparation going on, so I keep forgetting to write up the diary. We've had lots of snow and I am worried that people won't to be able to get here on Friday. Everything is almost ready now… I think.

The Charity Auction

✦

A Special Night for Lucy

Sunday 1 February 2015

It is Sunday and I finally have a chance to sit down and write this diary entry. I am still buzzing from Friday night, which was a great success.

Tamara and I spent all day on the Friday at the football ground getting everything ready. Daddy stayed at home to look after you. Tamara was amazing and so helpful; I couldn't have done it without her. She even booked the day off work so that she could help me. I am so very grateful to her. She also made 200 cupcakes for the event. These were intended to be free on the evening, but someone suggested putting a donation tin on the table next to them, which was an excellent idea and the cakes alone raised over £150.

It was freezing on the morning of the auction and the football ground car park was like a sheet of ice. We had to do several trips back and forth from the cars to unload all the auction lots and raffle prizes. I felt sure I was going to slip on the ice.

The staff at the football ground were great and they even gave us lunch to keep our strength up. When the balloons were delivered it started to feel really exciting. We decided on blue, yellow and silver to match the colours of the Children's Hospital Charity. I was beginning to get nervous as I knew I wanted to take the microphone and thank everyone, but would I feel brave enough to do so? I wasn't sure how emotional I was going to be.

Sure enough, I only managed to get a few words out before I got a lump in my throat. It was quite overwhelming looking around the room and seeing all our friends, family, colleagues and some friends from the hospital, and thinking about what had brought us together. Bernie came up on the stage to help me and I quickly got myself together and started again. I still didn't manage to say everything I had planned to, and it probably all came out as a bit of a ramble. But I hope people understood that we were hugely grateful for their support and that our gratitude would last for ever.

Bernie Clifton was fabulous, as was Becky Measures of Peak FM, and everyone had a really good night. It was such a great feeling, knowing we were raising lots of money for the fantastic charities that have supported us. Amongst the auction lots were a Tiffany bracelet, Manchester United signed footballs, a spa evening for two at Eden Hall, Elton John goodies, a signed Gary Barlow print, a One Direction print, a weekend away in Brighton, a week away at Sycamore Lakes near Skegness (where Nannie works in the summer), a night away at a Sheffield 4-star hotel, a family photo shoot, the Waterbaby swimming course, Boolies bouncy castle hire, and much more. It was very exciting to see the auction bids creeping higher and higher.

The raffle prizes were just as exciting, especially having sold 5000 tickets to people all over the country, thanks to friends and family who live throughout the UK. We were able to have five top prizes – first prize was the £500 holiday voucher, second prize was an iPad mini, third prize was £100-worth of John Lewis vouchers, fourth prize was £50-worth of Marks & Spencer vouchers and the fifth prize was £50-worth of Boots vouchers. There were over 70 raffle prizes, including champagne, chocolates, hampers, art work, scarves and jewellery, so we had loads of happy winners. I never anticipated this degree of generosity from friends and family and from people we hardly know. It has been incredible.

Nannie made me laugh as one of our auction spotters. She was bouncing up and down, throwing her arms up in the air when someone placed a bid. It was very funny. Auntie Claire, my cousin Debs, Uncle Mark and my friend Sam were spotters too. Poor Uncle Ben got the job of typing up all the raffle ticket winners on the power point screen; he was tucked away in the computer cupboard for ages, but did a great job.

Sian, Sarah, Auntie Alison, Uncle Mark and Katie were a great help too, helping to sell raffle tickets and manning the prize table.

A few weeks ago, a lovely man contacted us to say he would like to donate a wooden train that he had made. He had made four of these for his grandchildren and he said that he was making train number five to donate to the charity auction. The train looked splendid on display and we ran a 'Guess the Name of the Train' competition to raise some more money. We raised well over £50 with this.

Probably one of the best auction lots were two signed footballs from the Manchester United football teams, old and new. These raised £250.

Another popular auction lot was a Tiffany bracelet. Benji's auntie, Lindsey, placed the winning bid. She will wear it on her wedding day.

So, it was a huge success and the grand total raised was £10,132.94. It is far more than I ever imagined we would raise. The eight charities will be delighted, I am sure. The four main charities will receive £2300 each and the four smaller organisations will receive £250 each.

And just to add to our celebrations, Daddy starts his new job tomorrow.

New Year, New Progress

✦

Good Results from MRI Scan

Monday 2 February 2015

Just you and me at home today. Daddy left the house for his new job at 5am this morning. He is going to be away Monday to Friday for the next two weeks and I know he will miss you terribly.

We went to hospital today for a check-up and the good news is that you are now making your own platelets… clever girl! That's one less thing we need to go back to hospital for.

We have also been given a date to have your feeding tube replaced with a PEG and to have your Broviac line removed. More steps in the right direction.

Tuesday 3 February 2015

I think you are finally getting over that nasty cold. We are seeing our friends, Sian, Ioan, Sarah, Oliver and Millie later today. It's an early start tomorrow for another MRI scan.

Sitting with you as you play, with the sunshine streaming through the lounge windows, I am sure I can see new strands of hair coming through on your head…

Wednesday 4 February 2015

You had an MRI scan, the first since the high dose chemotherapy. I am sick with worry when it is a scan day. We won't get the results till next Monday, when Daddy will be with me.

We got home about 3pm and you are still very sleepy. You went to bed just after 6pm, which is very early for you.

Thursday 5 February 2015

You are very tired, probably still fighting that cold virus. In fact, you slept till 7am – unheard of!

You've played a bit this morning but you were sick at 10.30am and the feeding tube came out. Roll on the 19th when you are having your PEG fitted and Broviac removed – no more nasal feeding tubes. Only 14 days to go...

Friday 6 February 2015

We had a trip to the bank today to pay in the auction money. Over £5000 in cash and coins! I don't think I've ever carried so much cash into a bank. I was scared we would be robbed.

Nurse Tracey came out to us today. The tube hasn't come out but it has shifted position and it could be sitting in the wrong place, which is very dangerous.

Sunday 8 February 2015

Not sick at all yesterday. That makes us very happy, although we get your MRI results tomorrow and I am feeling extremely anxious and cannot settle to anything.

A lazy day at home today. Daddy took you to the park for half an hour while I did some cleaning. You weren't out for long, as it is so cold, but you had a quick go on the swings.

Monday 9 February 2015

MRI results today and thankfully they were positive: no change from the last scan. We need to focus now on 'rehabilitation', as the consultant says. On the 19th you will have the PEG fitted and Broviac removed. We need to try to get you taking solids again.

I have booked the Center Parcs activities today that Jack and Molly have chosen to do. They are looking forward to our weekend away. The charity night is all over and the cheques have been sent off. I'm getting that itchy feeling to do something else now.

I have been asking friends and family, including Jack and Molly's schools, whether they would like to participate in a 'Wear a Hat Day' for 'Brain Tumour Day' on Friday 27th March. People pay £1 to wear a hat to work or school for the day and all the proceeds go to Levi's Star, one of the many charities that have supported us. Levi's Star is a small charity based in Wakefield, named after a little boy called Levi, who died from a brain tumour at just six years of age. 'Wear a Hat Day' seems an easy way to raise funds for the charity and we could raise a useful sum of money to say Thank You for helping us. I've had quite a lot of interest so far and I have been sending out posters and letters from Levi's Star.

Tuesday 10 February 2015

Daddy left for work in Bedford at 5am this morning. Sian has asked if we would like join her at our old baby group this afternoon. Think we will – we haven't been since last July.

Thursday 12 February 2015

Yesterday was a busy day, sorting and posting out Levi's Star 'Wear a Hat Day' posters to friends all over the country who had offered to help.

We have had a very special delivery today, another present from our lovely friend Tamara and her little boy Jake. She really does spoil us. She sent you some special balloons for being so brave. I think it is also to celebrate the recent good news about the scan. It was a big surprise and you love playing with the balloons.

Friday 13 February 2015

Daddy came home this afternoon and you were very excited to see him. Jack and Molly have gone with their mum to Cardiff this weekend to visit the Dr Who museum as a treat for Molly's birthday.

Saturday 14 February 2015

Happy 7th Birthday, Molly, and Happy Valentine's Day! Daddy has given me some beautiful flowers and a card. I gave him a book – not quite as romantic but it was something that he wanted. We went for a drive into the Peak District and had lunch at one of my favourite pubs, The White Lion at Great Longstone. We went there a few times before you were born, so this is your first visit. The meal was delicious. We'll book a table there for Mother's Day, and we'll bring Granny.

Sunday 15 February 2015

We had lunch out again today, at Matlock Farm Shop; you, me and Daddy. You were very good. You love people-watching – just like Mummy does!

Jack and Molly got home at 4pm. Molly opened her presents and cards. She loved the big Lego set that we bought for her.

Monday 16 February 2015

It was an early start for Daddy today, off to work in Clitheroe, in Lancashire. We went to North Wingfield baby group. We used to go there most weeks before you became ill. We saw lots of your friends, Ruby, Thomas, Fin, Benjamin and Chloe. It was good to see them again.

Tuesday 17 February 2015

We enjoyed a walk in the sunshine today, up to the park to ride on the swings. I'm thinking about our next visit to hospital on Thursday, and getting your bags packed.

Wednesday 18 February 2015

We went to visit the lovely Tamara and gorgeous Jake today. It's half term, so Jake was off school and we had lunch together. Jake said he wanted you to have one of the toys that he had when he was a little boy: a baking tray with lots of toy cookies. You seem to love it.

We picked up Molly's birthday cake, a 'Frozen' design (after the Disney film, 'Frozen'), ready for Saturday. You will be in hospital again that day, so we will have Molly's birthday celebrations in hospital – unfortunately.

Exchanging Feeding Tubes

✦

A Surgical Ward... and a Holiday

Thursday 19 February 2015

It is the day that we have been waiting for, when the feeding tube is finally removed, for good. It will be wonderful for you and for us. I'm a bit nervous about the PEG...

You woke up a bit grumpy and very sore, but were given paracetamol and Ora-morph. We are not allowed to start the milk until tomorrow.

> *A child is like a butterfly in the wind*
> *Some can fly higher than the other,*
> *But each one flies the best it can*
> *Why compare one against the other*
> *Each one Is different.*
> *Each one is special.*
> *Each one is beautiful.*

Friday 20 February 2015

We didn't have the best night's sleep but then we seldom do, here in hospital. We are not on M3 Ward this time, because you are not having cancer treatment. We are on one of the surgical wards, S2. I miss the nurses and familiar faces from M3; and it is actually quite different not being enveloped by the sadness and despair that you can't help but feel when you are surrounded by children receiving cancer treatment.

We have seen two familiar faces from when were on S2 in August last year; a teenage boy called Timmy and his mum. She bought you a card and present when you were first diagnosed. They live in Lancashire but have been to Sheffield a couple of times for various treatments. Timmy is disabled and very unwell. I have the utmost admiration for the way that his mum manages to cope. It was a pleasure to see her and Timmy again, and she was equally pleased to see us.

You've just tried your first bit of milk, and so far so good...

Saturday 21 February 2015

It is Molly's birthday celebration today. It is sad that we cannot be with them all day. Molly, Daddy, Jack, Granny, Uncle James, Uncle Mark, Auntie Alison and Katie are going ice skating; something that Molly has wanted to do for ages. They will come to the hospital for a picnic lunch that Uncle Mark and Auntie Alison have kindly organised. The 'Frozen' cake will be a surprise. The nurses have very kindly allowed us to use one of the side rooms so that we can all fit around your cot.

There is a chance that we might be home later this evening if the milk feeds are successful.

Monday 23 February 2015

We are now back at home and it is just you and me again, as Daddy is away at work again. I think I've come home with hospital germs as I've lost my voice. My knee has also started to hurt again, which isn't good. I had an arthroscopy on the 1st August last year, when you first started to get really sick and I remember how difficult it was to leave you. We had just spent one weekend in hospital at Chesterfield. Little did I know that just 10 days after that day surgery on my knee, we would be rushing you to Sheffield Children's Hospital. It seems that I have a large chunk of cartilage missing in my knee and eventually I will need a knee replacement. I am hoping there is something they can do before that. I've managed to get an appointment for this Thursday. You'll be with Granny.

Tuesday 24 February 2015

Another terrible night. You were up at 10.30pm until midnight, then up again at 2.30am and wide awake from 4 to 5.15am. At least you then slept until 8am, but I am exhausted. When are the nights going to get easier?

Wednesday 25 February 2015

I'm a bit worried about you this morning. You were sick not long after waking and you quickly became very sleepy and were napping again by 8am. It is what you used to do when you first became ill last year. You have a runny nose again, so I'm hoping it is just a cold. I still have a sore throat, so maybe we've both picked up some hospital germs. I hope you'll be feeling better by the weekend, as we're going to Center Parcs.

Friday 27 February to Monday 2 March 2015

We are at Center Parcs, Sherwood Forest, on the holiday gifted to us by Amy's Retreat Charity. We arrived at about 11am, had some lunch and a quick play in the soft play area, and then went to find our accommodation. It is a woodland lodge, with a very modern interior. We've already seen some geese, squirrels, rabbits. A very beautiful, but inquisitive swan came right up to the lodge window. You loved it, pointing and making funny noises when you saw the swan.

We had tea in the lodge this evening. I nearly had a disaster with the oven when the plastic trays started to melt – the rice went everywhere. Not a good start.

Saturday 28 February 2015

Molly went off early to the first couple of activities that had been pre-booked for her: a cupcake decorating class and then she had her hair braided. Jack did target archery and the 'Laser Quest' with his dad in the afternoon. We all went swimming together late afternoon. The pool was a little chilly for you, Lucy, although Molly loved it, especially when the wave machine started. Jack isn't so keen on swimming and even the delights of the Center Parcs pool with its flumes and wave machines couldn't entice him into the water.

You were sick this morning again and Daddy and I are both quite poorly. Just when we are on holiday.

Sunday 1 March 2015

The day began with more activities for Jack and Molly. Molly made a bear and a bird box, then we all went ten pin bowling. You are doing lots of bottom shuffling this weekend and getting really good at it. It is a delight to see.

We had a lovely Sunday dinner in one of the Center Parcs restaurants. Of course, you couldn't join in with the eating, but you played happily in the highchair.

Monday 2 March 2015

Today's itinerary includes crazy golf and indoor tennis before heading home.

We've had a great time despite not being 100 per cent fit.

Wednesday 4 March 2015

You were quite sick again yesterday, which was worrying. The nurse came to check your PEG and that's all fine. We're allowed to get it completely wet, so we can have splashy baths again!

From today, Mummy is officially a Phoenix Card Trader. It is a home-based selling business in greetings cards, gift wrap, stationery and accessories. I even have my own website. I want to use it as a means to donate 10 per cent of my total sales each month to a different charity. I would like to support as many of the cancer charities as possible, promoting a different one each month. I don't know how it will go – maybe I won't sell any cards at all – but it will be a new challenge and will keep me busy. The first charity will, of course, be Amy's Retreat, following our super stay at Center Parcs.

We are doing the school run today, which we haven't done for months. I'm looking forward to seeing a couple of the mums that I always used chat to, and I know they are looking forward to seeing you. They are Tracy, Gemma's mum, who has been so kind, giving you many little presents since you became poorly. Alyssa's grandma, Janet, is also keen to see you.

Thursday 5 March 2015

We went to hospital today for an Oncology Clinic check. You have been booked for a Videofluoroscopy, as food is still coming out of your nose when feeding. Sometimes you are sick immediately. Something is definitely not right. You haven't gained much weight, so we have a different milk to try, that has more calories and is much denser.

Saturday 7 March and Sunday 8 March

A courier delivered my new Phoenix Trading pack yesterday. We had a happy weekend at home with a bit of sunshine for a change. Loads of bottom shuffling by you. You still like to wake up at all hours in the night.

Monday 9 March

I don't always get time to write this diary now that there aren't so many days sitting around in hospital. So, that's a good thing.

Daddy is working in Scotland this week. We went to baby group this morning at Alice's View, North Wingfield. We saw Claire and Oliver and Amy and Chloe. Then we delivered a card basket to my hairdressers, Ryleighs, in Clay Cross. They were very generous at our charity night, giving three of the prizes. They have offered to help sell some of my cards. We also delivered some brochures to tell people about my cards. I've got three card parties lined up too now, one at the Smithy Pond pub, one at Kaz's house (Evie's mum from Water babies) and one at Sharon's house, a friend from work. It is certainly keeping me busy.

Sunday 15 March 2015

It is Mothering Sunday and I feel blessed to be sharing it with you. There were times in August when I thought I might never have this day with you again.

We took Granny to lunch at The White Lion at Great Longstone. Daddy helped you to buy me some very special presents and a gorgeous card that I will treasure forever. Thank you Lucy for making me the proudest Mummy ever... xxx

Wednesday 18 March 2015

You are undergoing the videofluoroscopy today. If they can find out what is going wrong with your swallowing we can hope to start you eating solids again. The consultant has said that the problem might be a change in some scar tissue formed when you had Mucositis, or maybe there is an obstruction of some sort. The worst case scenario is that you have some nerve damage that will permanently affect your ability to swallow.

Thursday 19 March 2015

The videofluoroscopy has revealed the cause of the problem. It seems that you have no swallow at all. The tracer material that was used to show the throat and swallowing movement went down only a short way and then got stuck. The muscle in your throat did not move at all. You aspirated a little of the material into your lungs. This is the worst news possible and we are afraid that there is permanent nerve damage resulting from the tumour and/or the chemotherapy. You will be referred to the gastroenterology team who will do further investigations.

'Videofluoroscopy'
A moving X-Ray image of swallowing recorded to show an individual's swallow in real time, slow motion or frame by frame. It is an essential diagnostic tool for the assessment and management of people with swallowing difficulties.

Friday 20 March to Sunday 22 March 2015

A whole weekend without you. You had Daddy, Jack and Molly to look after you. It was Sonja's 'Hen Do' in Bath and I couldn't miss it. She is marrying the lovely Mikey in April, in Cambridge. It was a fun time (we rode on Segways, and I particularly enjoyed looking round the Roman Baths) but one night away would have been enough. By Sunday morning I was desperate to come back to see you.

Monday 23 March 2015

Mummy's first card party. We held it at the Smithy Pond pub, kindly hosted by Nicky. As promised, we donated 10 per cent of the total sales to Amy's Retreat. It went well and lots of my mummy friends came. They have been so supportive. It's because of you and taking you to baby groups that I have been lucky to make such good friends. Many of them came to the auction night too, and offered several of the prizes.

Friday 27 March 2015

Yesterday you were 18 months old and today it is 'Wear a Hat Day' for Levis' Star. We have raised over £1300 for the charity, which is a terrific result. Lots of schools and workplaces got involved.

Family Things

✦

A Holiday, Work, a Wedding, Birthdays

Saturday 28 March to Saturday 4 April 2015

This week we went on our second holiday of 2015, a splendid week in the Cotswolds, courtesy of the owner of holidaycottages.co.uk. This wonderful company supported us at the charity auction and offered us this family holiday, which we would take when you were feeling better.

We had a lovely time together. The cottage was absolutely gorgeous, set in the beautiful Cotswold village of Great Rissington, close to Bourton-on-the-Water. The weather was pretty miserable most days but we got out every day, seeing Bourton, Stow on the Wold and Broadway. We visited a model village, a motor museum and a bird park. We took refuge on the worst wet and windy days with tea and cake in the many coffee shops. Our favourite was, of course, a particularly welcoming café called, 'Lucy's Tearoom'.

On the Friday we had a big day at Adam Henson's farm (Adam is a presenter on the TV show, 'Countryfile'). Auntie Claire, Uncle Ben, Emily and Thomas met us for the day at the farm. You had a fine time, seeing all the animals, especially the baby lambs. Some had been born just the day before and were very cute. I think Molly's favourite was the trampoline.

You were quite poorly for most of the week, particularly at night time. One evening your temperature spiked quite high and Daddy had to find a local pharmacy to try and find some Ibuprofen as Calpol wasn't making any difference. You were sick several times throughout the week and we were prepared to return home, until you began to perk up a bit. I am pleased we didn't have to cut short the holiday for Jack and Molly's sake. Let's hope our next holiday will be illness free.

Friday 10 April 2015

Today was 'the wedding of the year' for our good friends, Son and Mikey, and I was so pleased that you were well enough to be with us in Cambridge. I booked the hotel when we were in hospital in December and I just couldn't imagine you being well enough to come with us. But you were and it made the day even more special.

It was a glorious sunny day and Sonja looked stunning. You almost upstaged the bride, looking beautiful yourself. It was lovely to be able to dress you in a pretty little outfit. Everyone was coo-ing at you, quite understandably. I cried as I watched Sonja walk down the aisle with her mum, Nancy. I cry at anything these days and have done since you were born. Jen, Helen and I each did a reading. You were particularly well behaved during the wedding reception and you even managed some bottom shuffling on the floor after everyone had finished eating. We stayed in the hotel at the wedding venue and Daddy looked after you for the evening so that I could have some time with the girls. Sonja danced all night and Jen was on top form. It was a great night and by midnight I was exhausted and feeling guilty that Daddy had stayed upstairs in the room with you most of the night. I said my goodbyes and came to join you. The next morning we enjoyed an excellent breakfast and then headed home. It was a terrific weekend.

Monday 13 April 2015

Tamara and Jake came to our house for tea today. They were amazed to see how much you had changed since they last saw you in February. Jake delivered a cheque from his school for the money raised for 'Wear a Hat Day'.

Wednesday 15 April 2015

You are getting bigger and stronger every day and can get just about anywhere, shuffling along on your bottom. I have lots of videos of you shuffling around the house and I can't wait to show them to you in years to come. Molly sometimes joins in, and you love it. You can pick up some speed!

Tonight something very special happened. You stood up in the bath all on your own, holding on to the bars on either side of the bath. You pulled yourself up, all on your own, and stood up tall and strong. In typical Mummy style, I cried happy tears.

Friday 17 April 2015

Yesterday we had a play-date with Thomas and Katie at their house. You are almost as tall as Thomas. You'll be weighed again soon and I'm sure you have put on lots of weight.

We've been busy today delivering card baskets. This month's 10 per cent donation will go to Ellie's Fund. This is another charity that supported us when Daddy was out of work for the few months that you were in hospital. 'Ellie's Fund – Brain Tumour Trust' was set up by her parents after the death of 14-year-old Ellie Othick-Bowmaker. During the three years that she fought her own two brain tumours, Ellie helped to raise over £25,000, inspiring many people to join in. Amongst its other objectives, the Trust provides assistance to families who live in Yorkshire and Humberside who have a child undergoing treatment for a brain tumour. It is a small charity, but was a great help to us.

Saturday 18 April 2015

Mummy and Daddy had a rare night out to celebrate the wedding of our friends Katie and Rob, at Shottle Hall, not far from Belper. Granny looked after you for the night and you were absolutely fine – once she got you into bed. I think it was quite a late bedtime.

Friday 24 April 2015

Yesterday we had an Oncology Clinic review at the hospital with Vicki, the consultant. All the experts seem pleased with your progress. You have gained nearly 2lbs in just over a month, despite having a few nauseous days, so this is really good.

Mummy had another Phoenix cards party tonight, hosted by Sharon, one of her colleagues in Scunthorpe. It went well and it was encouraging for me to see so many of my colleagues there, all keen to support me. Sandra, my boss, has also been in touch. I might start thinking about a phased return to work…

Friday 1 May to Friday 4 May 2015

Bank holiday weekend and you are here with Daddy. Jack, Molly and I are staying with Grandma and Grandad.

The nurse came to see us on Friday to give us a suction machine for use at home. Your secretions have been getting worse and when I mentioned it to Nurse Tracey, she suggested having the suction machine at home. You have particularly bad times at night so I think we need it. I can't help but feel sad that it possibly represents a step backwards. You had suction several times a day when we were in hospital in December. It is quite distressing to watch as you don't really like having it done, but I just have to tell myself it is helping you.

Tuesday 5 May to Monday 11 May 2015

You are teething, which is making you rather sick and raising your temperature. Gosh Lucy – you are doing your utmost to keep Mummy worrying.

I have started to think about the next charity night. I would love to repeat our success in January and if possible to make it an annual event. I think we should hold the next one in March 2016. I have been in touch with Chesterfield Football Club, who will give me a date once their fixture list has been finalised.

You are a little social butterfly at the moment, busy attending lots of 2nd Birthday parties. You have been to Eliza's at the Jungle soft play centre in Chesterfield, Henry's at Tibshelf village hall and next week it is Benjamin's party. As you know, Benjamin has the same birthday as me. We are hoping for nice weather as Benjamin's party will be outside at Grassmoor Country Park.

Tuesday 12 May 2015

We are seeing Sandra, my boss, today to talk about me returning to work. I stopped work nearly two years ago, when I took maternity leave. I did a few Keeping in Touch (KIT) days but have not been able to do anything else. As much as I want to get back to the routine of work, it feels quite wrong to leave you. You will have to come with me today as only Daddy and I know how to do the

PEG feeding. I guess we will have to train Granny if I am going to go back to work.

Wednesday 13 May 2015

It looks like Mummy is going back to work sooner than anticipated. I will take a couple of weeks' annual leave and then go into work on one day a week for a few weeks as a phased return. Granny has kindly agreed to look after you while I am away. It's starting to feel very scary...

We delivered a raffle prize to Chesterfield Royal Hospital today. I saw on Facebook that Macmillan are raising money to fund a new cancer treatment at the hospital. I particularly wanted to support their fundraising and have donated a Phoenix cards basket.

Saturday 16 May 2015 – Cards and Pamper Night!

Helen, Jen and Sonja have come to stay for the night. We had a 'pamper night', an at-home beauty session for we four and lots of Mummy's other friends. We will donate 20 per cent of sales to Macmillan and 10 per cent of my card sales. We had a great night and watching Jen, Helen and Sonja put their face masks on was very entertaining. Daddy was banished to the bedroom for the night. We raised over £100 in total for Macmillan, a very pleasing result.

Sunday 17 May 2015

It is Mummy's 36th Birthday. Gosh – I'm getting old! Daddy bought me a lovely silver Pandora bracelet and more charms, including a beautiful family charm, which is very apt.

Helen, Jen and Sonja left at lunchtime and you and I went to Benjamin's party at Grassmoor Country Park. It was a delightful party, and I was given my very own little cupcake for my birthday, made by Helen, Benjamin's mummy. When they sang 'Happy Birthday' to Benjamin, they sang it to me too. I felt rather embarrassed, since it was really Benjamin's party, not mine, but it was lovely thought by Helen.

It will be another big day tomorrow, with the gastroenterologists to see if they can do anything to help you swallow again.

Tuesday 19 May 2015

The gastroenterology clinic was extremely busy but after a long wait we saw the gastroenterology and the ENT specialists together. They will do an endoscopy to see inside your throat and your stomach. They will also examine your vocal chords and airways. There is a strong possibility of nerve damage, which will be irreversible, but they are hopeful of being able to help. We haven't been given a date for the procedure but it should be within six weeks.

We've another scan to get through first, the fourth of June...

Friday 22 May 2015

This afternoon we went to Matlock Farm Park with Becky, Ruby, Katie and Thomas. You loved looking at all the animals, especially the baby lambs and goats. We have bought an annual pass so that we can have lots more visits to the park.

Another memorable event happened tonight. I laid you down in your cot to sleep and next time I went in to check you were sitting up, playing with your toys. It's another sign that you are getting stronger and stronger – brilliant!

Saturday 23 May 2015

We went to the village of Crowle, near Scunthorpe, to watch our dear friend Tamara complete the 'Muddy Challenge'. She is raising money for one of the charities that have supported us, Ellie's Fund.

Tamara has already raised about £500 in donations on her 'Just Giving' web page for Ellie's Fund. She has been training hard for the 'Muddy Challenge'. I could never do it. The run was not at all straightforward. There were lakes and obstacles along the route. Before the run started she ran over to greet us and gave me a big hug. We were both in tears. On the back of her running vest she had written 'For my beautiful brave Lucy'. We took lots of photos of the day for your memory box. I am proud to call Tamara my friend.

Monday 1 June 2015

Mummy's first day back at work today and I felt so emotional leaving you. Granny looked after you all day. She is now fully trained with the PEG feeding and the suction machine. She is the best Granny ever!

Work went well but I couldn't hold back the tears on a couple of occasions; Donna gave me a big hug as I arrived. I think she knew how delicate I was feeling, and when I went to pick up my new laptop and phone the poor IT guys got more tears. They asked how I managed to have two years away from work and that set me off. I felt so silly and embarrassed because I never intended to make them feel awkward. I must try harder to hold back these tears.

I think I was particularly emotional today, not just because it was the first day back at work after a long absence, but also because it is the MRI scan on Thursday and I can't stop thinking about it. We won't get the results until Monday, so a very long weekend of waiting lies ahead...

Thursday 4 June 2015

The MRI scan was done today. Everything went well and now we just have to wait. You were very sleepy after being in theatre and it took a while for you to wake properly. You were fast asleep cuddling 'Cow Cow' for some time. Imogen was in theatre today for her regular treatment for Leukaemia and we saw them in recovery afterwards, which was good. You and Imogen are the bravest little girls I know. You have been through so much together – horrible times that little girls should not have to endure.

Sunday 7 June 2015

I tried to keep busy all weekend to take my mind off the scan results but with limited success. We had a fun afternoon at Clumber Park with Jack and Molly. I don't know why but this is the most anxious I have felt about scan results.

Monday 8 June 2015

It's good news! As soon as Vicki saw our anxious faces, she beamed at us and I knew what that meant. I was so relieved, I cried…again.

The small amount of the tumour that could not be removed by surgery remains present but it has not changed or regrown. That is good news and reinforces our general view that you are recovering well. I think I knew it would be OK, but I had to hear it from Vicki.

To celebrate we stopped off at Toys R Us on the way home and bought you an early birthday present. It's a pinky-purple trike, just the thing for summer. You look fabulous in it and it is so much better for walks than the boring old stroller.

Tuesday 9 June

My second day at work was just as tearful as before, but you were safe with Granny. It's lovely that you recognise her and give her a big smile when you see her. She's an expert with the PEG and I trust her completely to look after you. That still doesn't make it any easier to leave you.

Wednesday 10 June and Thursday 11 June 2015

Two days at home together. A couple of walks out in the sunshine together with you on the trike. Perfect.

On Thursday our physiotherapist, Denise, came to see you and was impressed with how well you are doing. You were kneeling up, standing, holding on to things and doing lots of bottom shuffling. You can now walk and take a few steps if we hold your arms. Amazing! You're a bit wobbly and can manage just a few steps but it is a great start. I am so proud of you and how far you have come these last few months.

Friday 12 June 2015

I am going to London for the night. My friend Louise bought me some 'Take That' tickets for tonight's show at the O2 Arena. Granny will look after you until Daddy gets home. I'm looking forward to seeing Louise as I have not seen her for over two years. It will be lovely to see her but I can't say I am looking forward to leaving you.

Thursday 18 June 2015

I hesitate to tempt fate, but life is slowly beginning to feel more normal at home. Our visits to the hospital are now fewer. However, we will return to hospital tomorrow for an appointment at the Hearing Clinic. One of the side effects of the chemotherapy drugs is possibly to damage your hearing. We have not had any indication of this, and the tests tomorrow are just precautionary.

Hearing and Swallowing

✦

More Unwelcome News

Friday 19 June 2015

The hearing test produced results that I wasn't expecting, that you possibly have moderate hearing loss. What else will be thrown at you? Haven't you had to deal with enough? I know it's no big deal in the scheme of things but it just feels like it's one more thing for us to cope with, something else that will require more hospital check-ups etc. We were told that hearing aids nowadays are very discrete and … I didn't really want to hear that today. I just feel disappointed that you could have one more thing to deal with and it's another long term issue.

Sunday 21 June 2015

Father's Day, and we have had a lovely lunch out to celebrate Daddy's special day. We went to the Peacock Inn at Owler Bar, near the Longshaw Estate in the Peak District. As always when we eat out, I feel so sad that you can't eat with us. We feed your milk through the PEG (and by now I'm used to people staring at us) but there is nothing else we can give you. It is too dangerous even to try, as you might aspirate food directly into your lungs. I can't pretend that I don't think about the other 21-month-old children who would be eating all sorts of things by now. I so long for the day when we can all sit round a table and you can tuck into the meal with us. It must happen one day.

Monday 22 June 2015

You've had a really sickly day, and you have been getting sicker these last few days. We have had to stop your medicine, Lansoprazole, ahead of the Endoscopy next week, which helps reduce the amount of stomach acid you produce. I didn't particularly think you needed this drug anymore, but you clearly do because of the effect on you without it. I can't think of any other reason why you would start being more sick…well I can…but it can't be that, I keep telling myself. It is not long since your scan, so all must be fine…surely?

Friday 26 June 2015

Today is 'Make it Better Day', a fundraiser for The Children's Hospital Charity. Our friend, Benji , is their poster boy and he is plastered all over the walls at the hospital, in the park, on the billboards outside the hospital. I'm not surprised that they chose Benji – he is absolutely adorable. One of his aunties, Katy, has offered to donate £2 for every selfie taken with Benji on one of these posters or leaflets.

Saturday 27 and Sunday 28 June 2015

Daddy has been away this weekend in Scotland, mountain biking with Uncle James. The weekend was booked last year but was cancelled when you became unwell, so it was well overdue. They had a great time. I think Uncle James was tired out with the biking, and then he had to drive all the way home.

You've been nauseous all weekend. It is so hard not to panic, seeing you so ill and waiting for answers tomorrow.

Monday 29 June 2015

You had an endoscopy today, which involved both the 'gastro' and the ENT doctors. I was hoping they would find something, as that might point to some remedy. The worry is that there is nerve damage from either the tumour or the chemotherapy treatment. Nerve damage could possibly be irreversible. Another possibility is that there is scar tissue causing any obstruction in the oesophagus. The tissue might then need to be removed.

We had another trip to the operating theatre, along with Cow Cow. Mummy did her usual thing and cried as she watched you being put to sleep. I still hate it as much as I did the first time. It happens so quickly, but today we had something extra to deal with. While you were still awake, the ENT doctor wanted to take a look at your vocal cords. They swaddled you in a blanket, which made you cry straight away, and I had to hold you tight while they pushed a camera instrument into your mouth. You absolutely hated it and I did too. I wanted it to be done quickly and for the thing to be removed. The ENT doctor was able to tell me straight away what he found: the vocal cords on your right side seemed to be a little weaker than the left. This was the last thing I wanted to hear, as it would imply nerve damage. When you were in post-surgery in August 2014, it was the right side of your body that displayed some weaknesses. Trying to reassure me, the doctor said that it might have minimal impact on your vocal cords. The left side would develop so as to compensate for the weaker right side.

You were in theatre for about an hour. Daddy and I went to Starbucks, which is right next door to the hospital. You often see families in there, sitting with a pager on their table. I completely understand their anxieties. Today it was our turn. Daddy and I hardly spoke. Think we were both just so anxious about what the endoscopy might find.

After about an hour we became impatient and walked back to wait outside the operating theatre. It was not long before the pager buzzed. I gasped and rushed into the waiting area with Daddy as one of the nurses came to meet us. Before we even stepped into the recovery area I could hear your little whimper. You are often still asleep after anaesthetics, or sometimes awake but very sleepy. Today you were really quite grumpy and obviously feeling upset. I was worried you were in pain after having that camera shoved down your throat.

We rushed over and gave you a kiss but you didn't really want one. You were clearly uncomfortable. I asked if I could pick you up and straight away you snuggled into me and rested your head on my shoulder. Within seconds you had fallen asleep again. Bless you.

As soon as I knew you were comfortable my mind began to race. I knew that the nurse looking after you would have been given a handover from the doctors and that she was ready to tell us we desperately wanted to know. Had they found anything? Did we need to stay in overnight? The nurse was kind, patient and reassuring. She said what she could to reassure me and that the doctor would be along shortly to talk to us. I should try not to worry. You would be taken up to a bed on S1 Ward and the doctor would see us there.

Sure enough when we arrived on the ward we were greeted by a nurse who recognised you straight away. You have established quite a reputation for being a 'bit of a cutie pie'. She commented on how much older you looked and said "Wow, look at that hair!" which warmed my heart. It was lovely to hear. I guess that seeing you every day I don't always notice the changes. This nurse hadn't seen you since February and she saw all the changes. With the constant emphasis on weight gain I always worry that you are not growing very much, so this was good to hear.

Soon, Dr Campbell came to talk to us. You were still snoozing on my shoulder, which was very considerate of you as it meant I could talk to the doctor. He explained that you had a hiatus hernia and that this was presenting severe gastroesophageal reflux disease. The sickness was undoubtedly caused by the build-up of stomach acid and the movement of it up and down your oesophagus. This would cause a burning sensation, possibly inflammation and general discomfort. I could feel myself welling up again. To hear that you were still suffering seemed so unfair.

Dr Campbell briefly explained the procedure that you would need to have done. It would involve another operation and a possible hospital stay of four or five days. But this one procedure would hopefully make an enormous difference to you. He explained that your stomach was being squeezed up into your diaphragm. The 'valve' in your stomach that stops this from happening is so damaged that they need to try to create a new one from tissue inside the stomach.

The procedure can usually be done by keyhole surgery but the doctors don't think this will be possible for you. If successful, it will help relieve the sickness that you are experiencing and it might also help you to learn to swallow again. Apparently, you have probably learnt not to swallow because it would be so painful to do so. There is still a chance that there is some nerve damage but we won't know more until the stomach procedure has been undertaken. Then they will review your ability to swallow, with another videofluroscopy. If this shows you have some swallowing capacity, however weak, there would be hope that you might be able to learn to swallow fully again. All scenarios will involve a long journey ahead.

I am disappointed to hear that you will need another operation, after you have already endured so much, but Daddy and I are relieved to know that there is a possible solution, and a definite plan of action. Unfortunately we now have another long wait for an appointment with the surgeon, who will plan a date for the procedure. They say that the worst case is possibly a delay of up to ten weeks to see the surgeon for the initial consultation and then up to a further six weeks before we will get booked in for the procedure.

It looks like we are not going to see you eating birthday cake in September. I will amend my dream slightly to Christmas cake…

On a more positive note we didn't need to stay the night in hospital and were home by 9pm that evening. We were a bit mean and tried to keep you awake on the journey home so that you would sleep when we got in. The plan worked. After a quick wash and a change into pyjamas you were more than happy to have snuggles and quickly fell asleep. Another exhausting day for all of us, and especially for you.

Dorset, Days Out, Fundoplication

✦

A Book for Lucy

Tuesday 30 June 2015

For the last few weeks I have been mulling over an idea to turn this diary into a book for you. I could perhaps type it up and then get somebody to publish it? Maybe this is a crazy idea but I'm going to have a go at it. I have also been thinking of ideas for our second charity night in March, and how the book idea might fit into that. Maybe I could aim to have the book finished in time for the charity night?

I did not share my idea with anyone at first, as they might have thought I was being a bit silly, but when I first mentioned it to Daddy, he thought it was a good idea. Then I told Nannie and by the time I had words of encouragement from Auntie Claire, Tamara, Helen, Jen and Sonja, I decided to do it.

I found a helpful publisher at Bannister Publications in Chesterfield, who approved the first 5000 words. He said it would be a compelling read and a story of love between mother and daughter. I hope when you read the book you will agree, and that you will forgive me for retelling your story. I know that you'll understand that my main wish is to raise money for PACT, who have launched an appeal to fund a new oncology clinic at Sheffield Children's Hospital. But I am also so incredibly proud of you, my little girl, for all your bravery and resilience. I want everyone to know about your journey and how brave you have been.

There is very little background material on ATRT. It is a newly diagnosed tumour, and only in the last decade or so have oncologists known how to tackle it. Previously it was often mistaken for another tumour, Medulloblastoma.

ATRT (atypical teratoid/rhabdoid tumour) is a very rare, fast-growing tumour of the brain and spinal cord. It usually occurs in children aged three years and younger, although it can occur in older children and adults.

About half of these tumours form in the cerebellum or brain stem. The cerebellum is the part of the brain that controls movement, balance and posture. The brain stem controls breathing, heart rate, and the nerves and muscles used in seeing, hearing, walking, talking and eating.

ATRT may be linked to a change in a tumour suppressor gene called SMARCB1. This type of gene makes a protein that helps control cell growth. Changes in the DNA of tumour suppressor genes like SMARCB1 may lead to cancer.

Because ATRT is fast growing, signs and symtpoms may develop quickly and get worse over a period of days or weeks. Signs and symptoms can include morning headache or headache that goes away after vomiting, unusual sleepiness or change in activity level, loss of balance, lack of coordination, or trouble walking and a possible increase in head size (in infants).

When you search online you discover the most depressing and heartbreaking stories. You are not going to be one of them, Lucy! I think we've got the better of this monster and the worst times are behind us. Maybe I'm being a bit too optimistic, but if other parents of children with ATRT were able to read this book it might give them that glimpse of hope that I so desperately searched for when you were first diagnosed. Above all that, you are the most important person who I want to read this diary.

My handwritten notebooks are tucked safely in your memory box, as they were originally intended just for you, but hopefully you will now be reading them in a proper book. I have sent a Facebook invitation to all of my friends to say that I am aiming to have it ready for the Charity Night on 19th March 2016, and to ask them if they would like to pre-order a copy. In just 24 hours I have had over 90 people say they would like a copy. I need to be able to sell

2015 - Fundoplication, Better Times and Good People

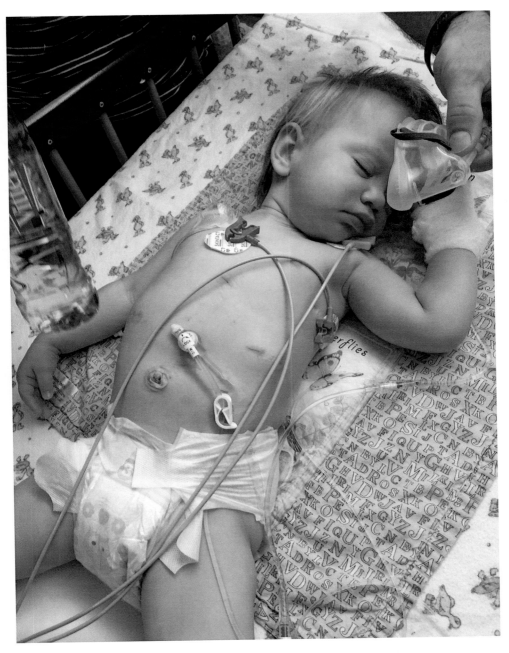

Recovering on the Intensive Care Unit after your Fundoplication procedure. You needed quite a bit of help with your breathing and so we were admitted to the ICU rather than the usual surgical ward.

Your first lick of an ice cream!
You were unable to swallow but
you were still keen to try some.

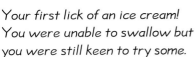

Left: Your first Steam Train Ric
from Corfe Castle to Swanage.
You were given a special ticket
to keep in your memory box.

Facing Top: Three of the
wonderful nurses from M3: Poll
Maxine and Claire.

Facing Below: Tamara and Jake
came to visit one evening to
present us with their cheque for
Levi's Star charity. Jake's schoo
raised the money with the 'Wea
a Hat Day' campaign.

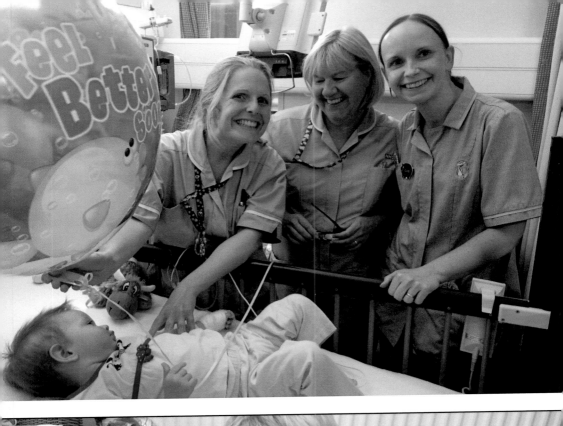

Left: Karen, one of the Recovery Nurses who looked after you several times after your operations, and has come to know you very well. She has become used to Mummy's tears.

Above: Jeanne, your wonderful dietician. The lady with whom we have had so many conversations about milk feeds, vomiting and NG tubes!

Left: Tracey Twyman, our community nurse from the Chesterfield team. An incredibly compassionate lady who has been our rock.

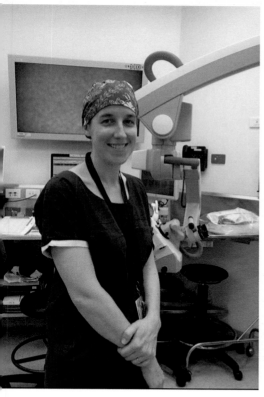

Above Left: Patricia de Lacy, one of our neurosugeons. We have so much to thank her for.

Above Right: Dr Vicki Lee, your Oncology Consultant. An amazingly knowledgeable specialist who, in our eyes, has saved your life. Her patience, care and understanding has seen us through our darkest days.

Right: Jack, Molly, Lucy and Katie: all the Needham cousins together, celebrating your second birthday.

Beryl Welburn, Coordinator for PACT.

Rachel Ducker, our community nurse and key worker from Sheffield Children's Hospital. Our 'Mother Hen'.

Clockwise from top left: Grandad Geoff,
Auntie Sam, Nannie Evison, and Nanna Kaz.

A very proud Mummy with her beautiful little girl, celebrating your second birthday, before the guests arrived. The birthday that we feared might never happen.

a few more than that to make it worthwhile, because there will be production costs that will need to be covered, but I would like to give PACT a generous donation.

So, on with the diary and on with the typing. I think your 2nd Birthday party might be the perfect finale for the book.

Thursday 2 July 2015

You have been sick three times today. If we hadn't had the recent endoscopy results we would be panicking again. Nonetheless, we have the possibility of two or more months of more sickness until you have your next operation. Please, please let's hope we get a letter in the post soon with an appointment.

My diary entries are less frequent these days. There isn't always time, now that I am back at work on two days a week. Granny looks after you on these days and you love being with her. I enjoy being back at work but it still feels very strange after almost two years away. I seem to have lost an awful lot of confidence. I am lucky to have many supportive colleagues, but Scunthorpe seems so far away. I hate that feeling of driving away from you each time I set off for work.

I am still selling the Phoenix cards and have a stall at Whitecotes Primary School Fair this Saturday, and another the week after at Arrow Farm Craft Fair near Worksop. The last craft fair sale was in Chesterfield a few weeks ago. It was extremely slow. I hope this Saturday will be more worthwhile – at least to make up for missing a whole day of playing with you. Despite the occasional setbacks, we have been able to make donations to Amy's Retreat, Ellie's Fund, Macmillan and Brain Tumour Research. The focus will now be on PACT for the next few months, helping them to raise funds for that new ward.

Friday 10 July 2015

We had a day out with Benji and Louise at Wentworth Garden Centre and Farm, near Rotherham. It was good to see them out of hospital for once – we haven't done so since we first met in the hospital last summer. You loved seeing the animals, happily pointing and waving at them. You were so well too. You have been much better on Lansoprazole, at double the dose now, and the sickness has gone. Hooray! It's time to start fattening you up! You still need suction a couple of times a day and we take the equipment with us in the car wherever we go.

Benji wasn't feeling quite as well as you, because he is still on his treatment. Leukaemia treatment has a much higher success rate than your tumour but the downside is that it takes about three years. Girls tend to have fewer relapses in treatment than boys, so they can often finish treatment a year earlier. Benji is taking steroids this week, which affects his mood and behaviour. I thought he was still as lovely as ever; I've seen far grumpier children who have never taken a steroid in their life. But I could sense that Louise was conscious of his changed behaviour, and he quickly became tired. Despite our worries, we had lots to talk about and we look forward to our next outing – maybe the next one will be steroid-free.

Saturday 18 July 2015

Jack is 13 years old tomorrow. Your big brother is getting really old!

We had a birthday tea for him with Granny, Uncle James, Auntie Alison, Uncle Mark, Katie and a couple of school friends. Tamara baked a 'Minecraft'-themed birthday cake that was a huge hit. They spent ages playing the game. Tomorrow he is going to 'Go Ape' at Sherwood Forest with his mum, Molly and some school friends.

Monday 20 July 2015

Today we finally met with the Gastro surgeon, Dr Lindley. We weren't there very long, just to confirm that he would proceed with the surgery and that he hoped to have a date for us within six to eight weeks. I just wish it could be sooner as it sounds like the procedure could help you so much.

It is called a Fundoplication and the surgeons basically create a new valve in the tummy. This will prevent stomach acid leaking up and down your oesophagus.

It is really quite sore and inflamed so until this is healed you won't be able to even try and swallow again. Let's hope the letter comes through in the post quite quickly with a date for the operation.

Tomorrow you and I are going on to stay for a couple of days with Nannie, just outside Skegness. You haven't been to Skegness since last summer, when we saw Auntie Claire, Uncle Ben, Emily and Thomas. You became very lethargic and were quite poorly. We will see Auntie Claire and the others again, and also my cousin's little girl, Isabelle. She was born a couple of months before you and we'll be there for her birthday. I'm sure that we'll have a good time and that you'll enjoy a playing on the beach, if the weather stays fine. We might even have a day together at Butlins.

Tuesday 21 July – Thursday 23 July 2015

We had a lovely time at Nannie and Grandad's house. We managed to meet Helen one afternoon in her lunchbreak and as hoped, managed a day at Butlins with Nannie, Auntie Claire, Uncle Ben, and cousins Emily and Thomas. I hoped you might manage a swim in the pool with Emily and Thomas but this was when you decided to have an afternoon nap – typically! We had a lovely day though, and you enjoyed watching the Barney show and Mike the Knight.

The BBQ at Auntie Angie's went ahead as planned too and it was great for everyone to see you looking so well and such a contrast from this time last year. Instead of making me look back with sadness at what happened last year, it made me realise how far you have come and I am incredibly proud of you.

Saturday 8 August 2015

We began our week in Dorset: the much anticipated holiday that we did not manage to have last year. As we packed the car on the Saturday morning, the sun was shining and the week ahead held so much promise. The M5 was horrendous, as usual, in the midst of the summer holidays, but we took a detour and enjoyed a lovely scenic route for the last hour or so of the journey. Mr Tesco was there, ready and waiting as we approached the cottage, so we knew our tummies would be satisfied for the week.

The weather was glorious that Saturday but unfortunately it didn't last. We had just one sunny day and we made this our day on Lyme Regis beach. The other days were either cloudy or rainy, although not particularly cold. Molly was looking forward to playing on the beach, building sandcastles and splashing in the waves. You weren't too sure about the sand at first and didn't seem to like the texture of it on your feet. Maybe the next time will be a more pleasurable experience for you. Daddy showed you his ice cream and to our surprise you went to take a lick at it. You didn't swallow any and it dribbled out of your mouth, but at least you were keen to try it.

Every day we made sure we got out and about and explored as much of Dorset as possible, even on the wetter days. It is a beautiful county, so diverse with rugged coastline and lush green rolling hills. We explored Weymouth, including the Sea Life Centre, which was fantastic and one of your favourite days I think. You were enthralled by the seahorses, turtles, and sting rays.

The famous Durdle Door and Lulworth Cove were definitely worth a visit and we enjoyed seeing these beautiful landmarks. We also visited the Tank Museum one rainy day. Not particularly my favourite day but Daddy and Jack certainly enjoyed it.

By coincidence, lots of my family were also in Dorset this week, staying at a holiday park near Bridport, a few miles further up the coast. We saw them on the Sunday and enjoyed a lovely tea with them in the evening. Last time they saw you was at the BBQ last year, and so it was nice for them to see you looking so much better.

Wednesday and Thursday brought back emotional memories of last year as it was on the Wednesday that the tumour was discovered on a CT scan; and Thursday was exactly a year to the day since you had the major operation to remove the tumour. I tried as best I could to forget and concentrate on how far you have come, but I can't pretend it wasn't on my mind. I am very pleased we decided to come away this particular week, and that we chose to do something that was completely different to where we all were this time last year.

The final day of our holiday was overcast and the rain clouds followed us most of the day. However, we made sure we made the most of it and enjoyed a stream train ride from Corfe Castle to Swanage. You were given your own special ticket saying 'My first train ride'. I loved it and although you weren't interested in a ticket, it will be a special momento for your scrapbook. Swanage is a charming little coastal town and we time for a stroll before returning to Corfe.

And then it was time to travel back to Chesterfield. Why do holidays always go so quickly? It was a fun, family holiday and the first time that you've actually seemed really well. You were sick a few times but nothing like how poorly you were at Center Parcs or the Cotswolds.

One lunchtime we were sitting in a pub and you were a bit snotty and dribbly because of your lack of swallow. A dear old lady suggested I rub some Vicks ointment on your feet, saying "It can work wonders". I just smiled and nodded politely. Bless her, what else could I say? You look like you permanently have a cold and we are constantly having to mop away your dribbles and runny nose. We took the suction machine with us everywhere and used it a few times each day, but you coped really well. I hope the Fudoplication operation makes a difference and that all these problems will improve once you start to swallow again.

Life certainly doesn't feel normal. I don't think we'll ever have that luxury again, but the holiday was very special and an insight into what we can look forward to in the future. We will have fond memories of the week... here's to many more enjoyable family holidays, all five of us.

Monday 17 August 2015

Today was a day of mixed emotions. We headed to the hospital for your long awaited Fundoplication and to have your PEG replaced with a more discreet MIC-KEY feeding tube, which sits at skin level to allow more freedom of movement.

While we waited patiently in Theatre Admissions, we thought of our friend Louise, Benji's mum, who was doing something far more exciting that day. She has been raising money to do a parachute jump, which would take place today. She has raised over £2000 for Sheffield Children's Hospital Charity. Seeing the photos pop up on my Facebook newsfeed made me think of her amazing achievement. She loved every minute, it seemed. Benji will be so proud of her.

We arrived at the hospital at about 11.30am. You were weighed and measured before heading to Theatre Admissions. Despite all the recent sickness you have gained some weight and you have got a little bit taller.

Usually you are first or second on the list for theatre, because you've been a serious case, but today you were third on the list and it was 3pm before you finally got called to theatre. Initially we expected to be admitted to S1 Ward following the surgery, but after discussions with the anaesthetist and surgeons, it was agreed that you might need more intense support post-surgery should your secretions become problematic. It was anticipated that you would need stronger pain relief, which would make you drowsy and unable to control your own secretions. So it was suggested that an evening on HDU/Intensive Care might be preferable. We didn't want a repeat of what happened on M3 back in December. So although, it brought back memories of being on HDU last summer, I knew it was the best place to be.

Fortunately, the night turned out to be fairly uneventful. You were definitely in the right place though, as you needed suction and

'Fundoplication'

Fundoplication aims to prevent stomach contents from returning to the oesophagus. The operation is accomplished by wrapping the upper portion of the stomach around the lower portion of the oesophagus, tightening the outlet of the oesophagus as it empties into the stomach.

After a fundoplication, food and fluids can pass into the stomach but are prevented from returning to the oesophagus and causing symptoms of oesophageal reflux.

In most cases, a fundoplication can be performed by a pediatric surgeon using a small telescope and miniaturized instruments.

oxygen overnight. You also gave us a bit of a panic when your face turned a bright shade of red and you became noticeably flushed. It might have been an allergic reaction to one of the drugs used in theatre probably, but the reaction didn't progress so the doctors weren't too concerned. I think we managed to get a few hours sleep in the early hours of the morning, but it certainly wasn't our best nights rest.

Daddy appeared back on ICU at 7am to find me asleep in the chair and you peacefully sleeping in the cot. I think he thought we had been like this all night. If only! It is just a reclining chair for the parent in ICU and as you can imagine, it is very difficult to get comfortable.

The doctors came to see you in the morning and it was agreed that you could move to S1 later that morning. You would receive strong pain relief for the next 24 hours but then you should be okay with regular paracetamol. So, some good news to start the day.

Then, Dr Harris, the hearing specialist popped her head around the curtain and I took a deep breath. She was about to tell us that the hearing test performed in theatre yesterday had proved conclusive? Were you going to need hearing aids? It was the news we didn't want. She said that the test showed even more severe loss of high frequency sounds than first expected. This would require hearing aids to be fitted in both ears. I felt so sad at this new 'rest of your life' intervention. I know hearing aids can be discrete and might never bother you, but I was just filled with sadness and disappointment. I was over tired and probably was not thinking rationally.

A plan was agreed to get the procedure started as quickly as possible, having moulds created from your ears and the aids ordered. I guess it is just one more thing we will need to deal with. And we will, because as long as we have you with us, that's all that matters.

There was a lovely surprise while we were on S1, a visit from some of the M3 nurses, Polly, Claire and Maxine who all looked after you while you were on their ward over Christmas. They saw you then at your very worst so they were delighted to see you now. They couldn't believe how much your hair had grown and that you seemed so much longer. It was lovely to see them and to tell them about well you have been doing at home.

On the Wednesday morning, Vicki Lee, your Oncology Consultant, came to the ward to see you. We were supposed to have a routine Oncology Clinic appointment on Thursday this week, but when she knew we were in for the operation she just said she would see us on S1 instead. I felt disappointed you couldn't show off your impressive bottom shuffling and standing up against furniture, or holding my hands to walk, but I think she believed us anyway.

We discussed the results of the hearing test and she wasn't overly surprised as it is a known side effect of two of the chemotherapy drugs, Carboplatin and Cisplatin. There is also a chance that the initial surgery to remove the tumour may have affected your hearing – I guess we'll never know for sure. So I am beginning to come to terms with the fact you will need hearing aids permanently. Vicki and I both agreed that purple ones would look quite nice.

You had a much better night in hospital on the Wednesday and didn't need any support with oxygen. On Thursday morning, plans were made for us to go home, although at one point I thought we would be in hospital till Friday at least. But yet again, you've made a quick recovery and surprised us all. Before leaving hospital we had one more appointment in the hearing clinic to have the hearing aid moulds made, and we made the very important decision about what colour hearing aids to have. We chose purple. They will take a few weeks to arrive.

By late Thursday afternoon we were back home. Let's hope that's the last hospital stay we need to have for a very long time. We will be returning to the hospital for various appointments including a follow up with the Gastroenterology team, meetings with the Hearing specialists and Speech and Language, as well as the usual check-ups with our Oncologist and the Neurosurgeons, but no overnight stays for the foreseeable future – fingers crossed!

Reflecting on Family and Futures

✦

Progress for Lucy... and a Critical Emergency

Sunday 23 August 2015

While you were in hospital I spent a lot time contemplating my career. A couple of weeks ago I noticed a job advertisement for a Corporate and Community Fundraiser for a local charity, called Brain Tumour Research and Support across Yorkshire. I was really excited when I saw it, but leaving education and my career in North Lincolnshire would be a huge decision. I was a primary school teacher for 10 years and then for the last six years I have worked with the local education authority. Everyone at North Lincolnshire Council has been really supportive too and I feel I would be letting them down.

They have been very understanding too, since I've returned to work. I find it very hard to focus on my work nowadays and I just don't think my heart is in it anymore. Scunthorpe feels so far away and it is a good hour or more to get there when I travel to work. I hate feeling so far away from you.

Initially the fundraising role would be in Leeds, as the charity works closely with the hospital there, however they are looking to expand their work to Sheffield, so this would be much nearer home. I just know I would have so much passion for the fundraising job. I'm sure that it would not actually feel like work, because fundraising has become such a big part of my life since you were diagnosed that it is something that I do in my spare time anyway, whether it be planning the next charity night or becoming involved with other various fundraising events.

I sent off an application form and just left it to fate. I will find out on Friday 21st if I am to be called to an interview. The interview date would be 27th August. I would be so disappointed if I don't get an interview.

By late afternoon on the Friday I still hadn't heard from the charity and began to feel disappointed. Maybe I hadn't even been short-listed for interview. Then at about 5.30pm I received an email from the Charity Manager to say that the shortlisting wouldn't be completed until Monday morning and that they would be in touch then. So a weekend of waiting lay ahead.

We kept ourselves busy on the Saturday and you went to your friend Oliver's 2nd birthday party. It was lovely to see so many of the mums that have become our close friends. I'm glad we were preoccupied today as it is a year to the day since we received your diagnosis. I remember the day vividly.

Monday 24 August 2015

You were quite poorly today; not sure why. You had very thick green mucus in your nose (delightful!) and just wanted cuddles for most of the day. However, from about 4pm onwards you started to perk up and by the time Daddy got home you were full of beans and he probably wondered what I was panicking about. Maybe you picked up some hospital germs; I don't know.

At 6pm Tracey, the community nurse, popped round to change the water in the balloon of your new MIC-KEY feeding tube. It seems very simple and I'm sure we will be able to do it ourselves from now on.

You were much better by the evening and having slept for most of the day, by 9.30pm you were still wide awake and bottom shuffling all around the house. Just when Daddy has to be up at 5am tomorrow for work and it's his birthday!

I received some good news today. I have been invited to a job interview on 1st September. I need to prepare a pitch to a leading firm of solicitors in Yorkshire asking them to consider BTRS as their charity of the year. I'd better get planning! I'll ask Gemma from the Children's Hospital Charity to help me. She is their Community Fundraiser and was a great help when I was planning the Auction

Night. Maybe she will be able to give me a few tips.

The five of us were supposed to be going to Skegness for the bank holiday weekend, to see Nannie and Grandad and for a BBQ at Helen and David's house on the Sunday. We were planning to stay late on the Monday but it will now be better to come back on the Monday morning, even though would be a shame to cut the weekend short for Jack and Molly.

Tuesday 25 August 2015

Today was Daddy's birthday. We celebrated in the evening when we were all together. Most of his presents were themed around his love for mountain biking: new knee pads and a subscription to his favourite mountain biking magazine. I bought him tickets to see the comedian Michael McIntyre at Sheffield Arena in October. It will give is another chance to have a rare night out together. We also made a special trip to Chatsworth Farm Shop in the morning to pick up a fresh cream Victoria Sponge cake for him, one of his favourites.

We spent most of the day at the hospital for a planned appointment at the Hearing Clinic, to try one last time for some conclusive results. Although it has been agreed that hearing aids will be beneficial, it is still unclear how much of the loss is down to congestion and how much could be nerve damage due to the side effects of the chemo.

The tests today proved to be more informative than when they were done whilst you were under anaesthetic. They still show some high frequency hearing loss but not as bad as first thought.

We still hope that the hearing loss could just be temporary, and will clear in time as you start to swallow again. This could possibly take months and therefore it is important for you to have hearing aids as soon as possible so that the development of speech won't be delayed any further.

You will be two next month and should be forming more defined speech by now. You are babbling and vocalising a lot but still not making any clearly defined sounds. So, something else for you to catch up on but I have every faith you'll manage it.

We were able to see Louise and Benji briefly when we arrived at the hospital. Benji had been in the Haematology Clinic for his regular check-up as part of his Leukeamia treatment. He looked really well and it was lovely to see him.

Gemma from the Children's Hospital Charity has already emailed me a lot of information. She is being so helpful. The more I research it, the more I want to get this job. It will be sad to leave North Lincolnshire, but this new job would be the ideal next step in our lives.

Wednesday 26 August 2015

Jack and Molly were here this morning, while their Mum was at work. You were happy to play with Molly while I caught up on some work emails and did a bit more preparation for the job interview next week.

In the afternoon we visited our friends Kaz and her daughter Evie, who used to be in the same Waterbabies class as you. She is just a month older than you and had her 2nd birthday a week or so ago. We took her a little birthday present.

Daddy is working away in Wales today and tomorrow but will be home late tomorrow or Friday morning. He is working away more and more lately and doing so much travelling - its beginning to get him down. He oftens leaves at 5am in the morning and doesn't see you till he gets home from work. He enjoys the work but he's started to think about looking for another job without the travel.

Thursday 27 August 2015

It is a year ago today since you had your shunt fitted. During chemo and for a few months afterwards, until about March 2015, you had lost your hair and so the shunt was very prominent at the back of your head, but now you have a lovely full head of hair and I don't think the shunt is noticeable it at all. I sometimes forget it's there. Fortunately, you've had no problems with it: often they can get blocked or infected, or even stop working, which is potentially

133

life-threatening and must be rectified immediately in theatre. Any bump to your head is serious and we must check that the shunt hasn't been affected.

It is wonderful that we have reached this milestone of a year post-diagnosis. The medical statistics in the beginning suggested that we would never see this day. I love the way you've proved them wrong. You have been through so much and have overcome even more. We are incredibly proud of you. Of course, we shouldn't be over-confident, because the critical milestone will be the two-year point after treatment ends. And maybe I shouldn't dare write this, but I have a gut feeling that you are going to beat this for good. There will be obstacles to climb, such as your difficulty with swallowing, possible growth problems, and hearing loss, but as long as the tumour stays away, we will deal with anything else. There may be tears along the way, probably more from me than anyone, but as a family we will get through anything that is thrown at us.

I think about one of the other potential side effects, that the chemotherapy may well have left you infertile. Although you are now just my baby girl, it terrifies me that you might not be able to have a baby of your own. Knowing how much I wanted you, I'm sure that you will have the same desire to have a child of your own. I would be devastated for you if this were to become a problem for you. But there is always hope, as you may well be able to carry a baby, just not conceive naturally. In 25 to 30 years' time, when you choose to have a baby, IVF will have advanced even further, so who knows what options will be available to you. Maybe I shouldn't panic about such things so far ahead in the future.

Granny Sheena looked after you today while went shopping at Meadowhall. I was determined to find an evening dress for the Levi's Star Charity Ball that we are attending on 19th September. Granny will look after you for the whole night while Daddy and I stay over at the hotel. I'm a bit nervous about it, since it will be the first night since you were born that neither Daddy nor I will be there. I know Granny will be absolutely fine, but knowing how little you sleep I am worried you will keep her up all hours.

Friday 28 August – Monday 31 August 2015

Bank holiday weekend and we drove over to sunny Skegness. It has been a long time since the five have us have made the trip. Jack and Molly were excited to see 'Crazy Nannie Pauline' as they call her.

The sun was shining as we arrived and headed for the seafront. It was a bit cold and windy so we didn't play on the beach, but just walked along the seafront for ice cream. We went to the Fairy Dell paddling pools, where Molly was determined to have a splash around – no chilly weather was going to stop her. At about 5pm we made our way to Nannie and Grandad's house in Burgh-le-Marsh, wher we tucked into fish and chips for tea.

On the Sunday we were invited to a BBQ at our friends, Helen and David's house. They always host a BBQ on bank holiday weekend, regardless of the weather. It was no great surprise when the rain started and it did not dampen the fun. Everyone was pleased to see you. You were really well and played happily with Ella and Isabel's toys all afternoon.

By Monday morning the rain was coming down harder and we knew we weren't going to be able to enjoy anything outside. We drove up the coast to Mablethorpe to visit Grandad Geoff and Nanna Kaz and the rest of the Needham clan. They have a caravan and spend most of the summer there. They were delighted to see you and Jack and Molly, and it was another opportunity for some family snaps.

Late on Monday afternoon we were safely back home in Wingerworth. I unpacked and then worked on my job interview. I was unusually nervous about it, probably because I really wanted the job and would be so disappointed if I didn't get it. Daddy had to pack for a week's work in Liverpool. He had applied for another job in Alfreton; much closer to home and with much less travel. So hopefully, both Mummy and Daddy will have new jobs soon.

Tuesday 1 September 2015

Granny arrived at about 8.30am and I headed nervously out of the door to my interview in Leeds. You blew kisses to me at the door as I left and this made me smile. I felt sure they would bring me extra luck.

I think the interview went well, although you never know with these things. I was worried that I might get upset if I talked about you, and at one point I had to take a deep breath to stop the tears from rolling, but you would have been proud of me. The question was, 'What motivates you work for a charity such as Brain Tumour Research and Support across Yorkshire?' I just about managed to get the word 'Lucy' out. The panel already knew about you as I had mentioned what you had been through in my covering letter. I think they realised straight away that I wasn't going to be able to say much more without getting upset. I knew that the manager of the charity had lost her own father to a brain tumour and I felt an enormous sense of understanding from her. I came away feeling very positive about the interview and buzzing over the possibility of working for them. I'll be very disappointed if I am unsuccessful. They said they would be in touch by the end of the week, which was unusual; with teaching jobs you normally find out on the day of the interview.

Wednesday 2 September 2015

Today we are off to the hospital again to have your hearing aids fitted. I still can't help but feel a bit emotional about it. It is one more thing you will have for the rest of your life, something else to have check-ups for and something else to be careful with.

It was a long appointment with more tests before finally fitting the hearing aids. The purple ones hadn't arrived so you have some silver-grey ones that possibly look less obvious than purple ones. It was wonderful seeing your reaction to my voice once they had been inserted and you definitely seemed more alert and appeared to be listening to different noises as we walked out of the hospital and back to the car.

The doctors mentioned the possibility of another procedure. They think it might be beneficial to have some Grommets fitted to help clear the fluid that is congesting your ears. The audiologists will refer us back to the ENT specialists, who will make the final decision. And I really thought we might have a rest from anaesthetic for a while…

Thursday 3 September 2015

Just you and me at home today. I hate waiting to find out about the new job, I am so impatient!

The hearing aids don't appear to be disturbing you although they are squeaking an awful lot. I wonder if this is normal? You seem to be more engaged with the television, especially 'Mr Tumble'. Maybe you can hear more. It must feel strange to hear lots of new noises.

The Fundoplication procedure has had absolutely amazing, instant results. You haven't been sick once since the operation. It is wonderful! Sometimes you retch a little after a big feed but the surgeon said that might happen. Occasionally we have to release a little bit of air using the syringe connected to your button. The MIC-KEY button is much better than the PEG tube, and considerably easier to care for. The dangly PEG tube used to get in the way when you were playing, but with the new button we can simply detach and re-attach the feeding tube.

Sleep is still something we are working on. You rarely sleep all the way through the night. Daddy and I are constantly tired. You often have a long nap in the day so you manage to catch up on some sleep, but then Daddy and I don't. I'm sure this won't be forever and things will calm down soon. Sometimes you are awake for two hours at a time in the night. Little monkey you are! But always full of kisses and cuddles.

Friday 4 September 2015

I waited anxiously at work for my phone to ring. At about 3pm I got the call I had been waiting for. My heart just sank when Rachel, the Charity Manager, said "You've not been successful for the role we interviewed you for," but then quickly added, "however..."

...and it was the best news! Rachel explained that the interview panel had been very impressed with my presentation and with my experience and contacts in Sheffield. They would like to create a new role for me, fundraising in the Sheffield area and creating links with the hospitals in Sheffield on behalf of BTRS. The charity is not well known in Sheffield, as much of its work is in Leeds. However, as a Yorkshire charity, they would like to generate more exposure in Sheffield.

This just sounded too good to be true – just the perfect job for me! You gave me a big smile and a kiss when I arrived home from work and I'm sure that was your way of saying 'Well done Mummy'.

Saturday 19 September 2015

The Levi's Star Charity Ball, at the Cedar Court Hotel in Wakefield. Daddy and I had our first night away together since you were born. We left you in the good care of Granny, and two A4 sides of my notes to read through. Jack and Molly were staying overnight too and I knew Molly would be a big help to Granny. She knows where everything is and will help Granny if need be.

Daddy and I were invited as special guests. We accepted on the condition that Levi's mummy also came to our charity evening. I had asked some of our friends to join us and we had a full table of ten. Despite a couple of friends having a bit of a nightmare journey on the M1, by 6.30pm the men were all suited and booted in their tuxes and the ladies were all glammed up in their long dresses. We had just finished our starter and the wine had just started to flow, when my mobile rang. It was Granny. I was sure she would only ring if something was wrong. I answered with an anxious "Hello, everything OK?"

"Tracey, I don't know what to do!" was her hurried reply. I ran out of the room into the foyer to speak to her properly. She said that the whole of MIC-KEY tube had come out. The whole thing! It left a gaping hole in your tummy. Arghhh! This had never happened before and we had been told that if it does come out, which it shouldn't, then you only had half an hour to re-insert it otherwise the hole can start to close up and you would need to go to theatre to have it redone.

What were we to do? We were an hour's drive away. Granny said that you had gone to bed on time and fell asleep nicely but then woke up a short while afterwards and Granny couldn't get you back to sleep, so brought you back downstairs. You still had the feeding attachment on (as we do often keep it on while you're sleeping so we don't disturb you when we feed you again at 11pm) and it must have pulled on something as you were playing with Molly. So, nobody's fault and just one of those things. It didn't hurt you and when it came out there was only the tiniest bit of blood. You weren't in pain, in fact I could hear you 'bah bah bahing' in the background as I was talking to Granny.

I decided that the out of hours community nursing team in Chesterfield would be the best people to call. I had rung this number hundreds of times before, everytime your NG tube needed replacing this is who we would ring. But because I was panicking I somehow kept ringing the office number rather than the out of hours mobile and couldn't understand why I wasn't being put through to the pager answer phone. Time was ticking so I rang the surgical ward at Sheffield Children's hospital and asked if I should ring 999 as I needed someone to come out to you within 30 minutes. We had already lost 10 to 15 minutes and were fast running out of time. They said I should ring for a paramedic. We just needed to get some sort of tube re inserted so that the hole didn't heal up.

I rang 999 and asked for an ambulance, something I've only done once before and this time it was for you. I tried to stay calm as I knew it wasn't an emergency in the sense that you needed help with breathing or anything, but I also knew if we didn't get the tube passed again you would be heading off to theatre and I really didn't want to have to put you through that again. I explained all this to the operator and she explained that she would send out a para-medic.

While I was worrying, Daddy phoned Granny to talk through what she could do if she would need to deal with the emergency herself. We had a spare kit upstairs for this sort of problem and Daddy knew what needed to be done. He just had to tell Granny what to do, whilst trying to stay calm, with one phone on her shoulder and looking after you, all at the same time.

In the meantime, I decided to ring the community nurses again. This time I got through straight away to the pager answering system. I realised my previous mistake and couldn't believe how stupid I had been. It was Michelle, who of all the community nurses lived in Walton, just three miles from us. She had visited us several times in the middle of the night and early in the morning, to repass an NG tube and so she knew all about you. She is also very familiar with the MIC-KEY button and knew exactly what she needed to do. She set off for our house straight away. I explained that a paramedic may well be on their way too but she said she would still go as they might not be entirely familiar with the feeding tubes.

So as I came off the phone to Michelle, Daddy came off the phone to Granny and said that she thought she had done it, with him talking it through what to do. It is quite a tricky affair, having to carefully deflate the little balloon that sits inside your tummy, reinserting it into your tummy, and then inflating again with water, using a syringe. It would be very fiddly, especially if she was trying to do it one handed while holding you still with the other hand. I don't know how she did it but I am so grateful she did. What an amazing Granny you have.

It was a good job I rang Michelle because the paramedic still hadn't arrived by the time she arrived at the house and so we cancelled the request. I was now back on the phone to Granny and listening to what Michelle was saying in the background. I could just hear her say "No everything is fine, you've done it absolutely perfectly". The tube was testing fine, which showed it was inserted in the right place and they were managing to pull back milk into the syringe, so all was fine. Michelle then came back on the phone to me and I explained that we go home immediately, but she insisted we stay where we were and enjoy the night. She said that everything was absolutely fine and there was no reason at all to come back home and spoil our night. She would take a photo of you and your feeding tube so I could see all was well.

Daddy and I just sighed a massive sigh of relief. Of all things to happen on our first night away! A couple of minutes later the photos came through. Jack had sent them to Daddy's phone. You just had a big smile on your face.

We hesitantly rejoined our friends and debated whether we were doing the right thing by staying, but once we had seen the photos and spoke to Granny again, it was clear that there was nothing more to be done and that we might as well stay and try to enjoy the rest of the night.

It turned out to be a really fun night and everybody helped us to relax. The auction raised a fantastic amount for the charity. Vicky delivered an amazing presentation – very emotional and tears were streaming down my face listening to the statistics about brain tumours and the lifelong effects. Yes, tonight had been a drama, another one in our eventful lives, but it made me realise just how lucky we were to still have you with us. Levi's family had not been so fortunate and they have had to deal with the ultimate loss. It was a stark reminder of what brain tumours can do. We love you Lucy with all our hearts… xxx

Two Years Old

✦

So Much to Deal With...

Monday 21 September – Friday 25 September 2015

I have been very busy over the last couple of weeks sending emails and letters to various businesses and companies asking for donations for the next Charity Night in March 2016. I've had lots of success already and its getting really exciting. Donations have included free tickets to Legoland Discovery, Sheffield Wednesday home game, Jorvik centre, Sunday lunch for two at the Cavendish Hotel in Baslow, £50 garden centre vouchers, two picnic hampers and much much more. All this from my first batch of emails!

I met with my new boss last Friday in Leeds. My new role with the charity feels so right. It was sad to hand in my notice at North Lincs but they were very supportive and understood my decision. I will finish at North Lincs around October half-term and possibly start my new role with BTRS in November. I really can't wait.

It is also time to start finalising the plans for the party of the year. Party bags have been made up, Tamara is busy preparing the cake and I have been shopping for bunting, balloons and party food. It is good to be finally planning this very special party for you – our gorgeous little girl will soon be two years old.

Saturday 26 September 2015 – Happy 2nd Birthday!

The big day has finally arrived! Today is your 2nd Birthday and we are going to have the most amazing party ever for you. We have booked Wingerworth Church Centre and Chuckle Chimps, the company that we had booked for you last year. They very kindly offered to provide the soft play, bouncy castle and a sweet cart, free of charge as a gift for you. Such kindness continues to overwhelm me and if nothing else, over this last year or so, my faith in humanity has been restored. Friends and family have been so kind and businesses like Chuckle Chimps, who don't even really know us, have been so generous. This is the same business that also offered a wonderful auction prize at the Charity Night last year. Sarah, from Chuckle Chimps, has already offered us the sweet cart, free of charge for our next charity night March 2016. Truly amazing.

The day began with the enormous task of opening all your presents from friends and family who weren't going to be at the party. It felt like Christmas Day all over again. There were presents of all different shapes and sizes and cards from many friends and family. I was very touched to see a card had arrived in the post from Patricia De Lacy – the neurosurgeon who first operated on you and broke us that terrible news over a year ago now.

Lots of our friends from our baby and toddler groups came to your party and they were all so excited to be there. You were invited to their 2nd birthday parties, but now it was finally time for you to be hostess. And what an amazing special hostess you were, so happy all afternoon. I was a little worried you might be a bit overwhelmed by all the different people, the bouncy castle, the soft play and all the balloons. But to our delight, you seemed to love every minute of it.

I so pleased that this day has finally come. It is a massive achievement to have overcome everything in this last year or so. You are just two years old today and you have had to deal with so much – more than any two-year- old should have to deal with. Yet you are still smiling. Mummy and Daddy are so very proud of you.

And so I think it is time for the diary to draw to a close. I am not sure I can keep up with it everyday, and I am hoping that life won't be quite as eventful from now on. I will just be happy with a 'normal' life, if that's possible. I desperately hope that the dark days are behind us and it is now about looking forward to what the future might bring.

The beginning of October brings us more anxiety as you are due your next MRI scan. I think they will continue at four-monthly intervals for some time yet, possibly increasing to six-monthly in the not-too-distant future. Eventually you will just have annual scans. I have to try to remember how well you are, rather than getting too anxious about the scans. That will always be easier said than done. November will bring the start of my new job with BTRS, so maybe things are finally starting to go our way.

The road ahead still has many unknowns and there are things that maybe a 'normal' two year-old would do that you can't quite manage. We will still be going to the Children's Hospital several times a year for various appointments and checks with the Hearing Clinic, the Gastroenterologists, Physio, Dentistry, the Neuro-oncologists and others.

We are still waiting for your very first steps, although last week you were slowly starting to cruise along the furniture in the living room. You are extremely wobbly, which Vicki has said would most likely be the case. The part of your brain where the tumour was affects coordination and balance. You are getting stronger by the day too, and you haven't been sick since the Fundoplication. This is hugely significant. For the first time since last August you have outgrown your nappies and have quickly gone from 9-12 months to 12-18 months clothes in just the last few weeks. Your face looks fuller and you are generally happy and content most of the time. This is all we can ask for. As long as the suffering is over with, we can try to deal with whatever obstacles come our way.

I think life will continue to throw various challenges your way but with Mummy and Daddy, Jack and Molly, holding your hand all the way, we will get there together. Stay strong, keep smiling that beautiful smile and don't let anything beat you.

We love you now and always Lucy, our very special, brave little girl... xxx

*'Whenever you find yourself doubting if you can go on,
just remember how far you've come.*

*Remember everything you have faced, all the battles you have won
and all the fears you have overcome.*

*Then raise your head high and forge on ahead,
knowing that YOU CAN DO IT!!'*